Fiona Talbot and Alexander Talbot
which4words

Fiona Talbot and Alexander Talbot

which4words

Business Writing for Humans

DE GRUYTER

ISBN 978-3-11-914443-8
ISBN 978-3-11-221769-6 (PDF)
ISBN 978-3-11-221770-2 (EPUB)
DOI https://doi.org/10.1515/9783112217696

Library of Congress Control Number: 2026935803

Bibliographic information published by the Deutsche Nationalbibliothek
The Deutsche Nationalbibliothek lists this publication in the Deutsche Nationalbibliografie;
detailed bibliographic data are available on the Internet at http://dnb.dnb.de.

© 2026 Walter de Gruyter GmbH, Genthiner Straße 13, 10785 Berlin, Germany

De Gruyter and Walter de Gruyter GmbH are part of De Gruyter Brill.
www.degruyterbrill.com

Questions about General Product Safety Regulation:
productsafety@degruyterbrill.com

Printing: CPI books GmbH, Leck

To family: Johanna, Leander and Colin, with love.
To all the team at De Gruyter Brill: with special thanks to Matthew Smith for his vision and enthusiasm.
We dedicate this book to you all.

Contents

Introduction

The ability to express oneself, to convey a message to others, to convince, to sell, to connect, indeed, to communicate generally, all come within the remit of business writing. So why is its importance so often overlooked or taken for granted, as a basic skill that everyone has already mastered?

Stop for a moment to consider that wherever we look:
- at the business minds of tomorrow in education today
- at people making their first steps in the business world
- all the way through to seasoned professionals
- and at those for whom writing can present particular challenges perhaps because of neurodiverse considerations generally or specific challenges such as dyslexia. (More on this in Chapter 6, with a powerful message from Theo Paphitis, Retail Magnate, and Dyslexia Empowerment Patron for the British Dyslexia Association.)

We *all* need help to navigate the busyness of today's world.

We're overwhelmed by information that's all too often completely ineffective. We're struggling to protect bandwidth and cut through the noise. We can see the benefit of embracing the help of AI tools but alongside this need to maintain our uniqueness as individuals, and as humans.

We're excited to introduce our brand new **which4words** method which is a leveller that should suit all learning styles. It's all about clearing your mind and then developing focus to:
- Help you organise and plan your writing
- Understand how a structured writing system lights your path
- Build confidence, relieve anxiety and writer's block
- Understand your audience and cut through the noise to get to your desired outcome quickly and effectively

And here we have our first **which4words** takeaway:
1. **Plan**
2. **Writing-system**
3. **Confidence**
4. **Results**

Follow us on the journey, as we guide you to communication success from the beginning to the zenith of your career via this book, designed to be your essential toolkit to make you a powerhouse of written communication.

© 2026 Walter de Gruyter GmbH, Berlin | https://doi.org/10.1515/9783112217696-001

The authors

Best-selling author and Business Writing expert Fiona Talbot and her son, International Business expert Alexander Talbot, share their communication and life skills, enriched by their experience of living and working abroad. Both understand how tailoring your communication pays immense dividends, both socially and in a business context.

Keen also to highlight how intergenerational and collaborative working demonstrates how much everybody can bring to the table, they pool resources to bring you this ultimate guide to effective business communication in the modern world.

With decades of theory, classroom learnings, workshop outputs as well as practical experience from all corners of the globe from small to big business, leading teams and managing stakeholder relationships from every level and step of the business value chain – all this offers a big reason for you to believe in this book.

Here's a snapshot of each.

Fiona Talbot

An internationally acclaimed author, facilitator, communication trainer and coach, Fiona specialises in Business English communication skills, and also effective business writing across the board. Her books (many translated into other languages) and articles in multiple business magazines and press, help individuals at all levels of their career, as well as businesses and public bodies of all shapes and sizes, and universities all over the world.

She is admired for her enthusiasm for the subject and desire to help people flourish by understanding how words chosen well are the route to sustainable communication success on what can and should be an enjoyable journey!

Alexander Talbot

Having spent two decades working at all levels up to senior executive level, from start-ups and scale-ups to some of the world's largest organisations, having lived in seven countries and worked all across the globe, Alexander aims to reflect the practical application of the **which4words** system. He provides examples from the field, as well as drawing on experience of running and leading teams, where the power of business writing skills is a key driver to success.

In addition to types of organization and global locales he has worked in most business areas: from marketing to technical functions, IT/IS to project management and finance.

His superpower is being able to find and assemble the right people, provide the right input/guidance and facilitate the output to achieve what may even seem to be impossible goals. Some call this innovation – for him it is just helping people to unlock their full potential.

Coupled with his passion for compass, direction, and self-development, he knows it's all about effective communication.

1 How the world of business writing has changed – and introducing the which4words approach

Here we introduce the background to writing and examine where we fit in the changing communication landscape today. In subsequent chapters, we'll be examining why effective writing matters, including its effect on productivity.

PART 1: Let's start with a constant – whatever the background, we're almost all business writers today

It's an inescapable fact that yes, you are a business writer the moment you have to write an email, an instant message, a sales pitch, a job application, a social media post, an invoice, a customer-facing message, a technical document, a public sector announcement, a legal document, a letter to a patient, and the list continues . . .

We're out to help everyone who falls into these universal categories, be they students or apprentices about to enter the workplace, or junior. middle and senior managers and CEOS.

The written word matters on oh so many levels; the digital landscape is changing everything for us all and people are getting overwhelmed by the volume of information constantly coming at them.

Bandwidth overload is fast becoming gripe number 1

There's simply not enough time in the day to sift through the reams of ineffective communication bombarding us. Getting to the point is vital for us as time-addled individuals.

This is:
- not only to manage our workload, but also
- to increase the chance of connecting with our equally time-addled audience

It's time to work out how to do this and the theme of the book is to help you seize the opportunity our new **which4words** method affords you to do that, by breaking concepts down into individual powerful words, to communicate clearly and succinctly in the modern world.

Once we get our heads around this need to get to the point, we can use Artificial Intelligence (AI) tools to help us with the 'heavy lifting' in so many of our business writing tasks. And as AI gets better at doing this, as it will, we will have to get better too and stay at the helm, so to speak, understanding that an equally important need is to ensure we still write as humans to humans.

So who is this book aimed at?

It's at everyone who wants to grasp the opportunity, both in terms of theory and practice, that these rather exciting new developments are creating:
- In occupational/professional terms think students, start-ups, sole traderships, small, medium and large organisations . . . think Science, Technology, Engineering and Mathematics (STEM), Civil Service, Supply Chain, Medical, Pharma, Finance, Customer Service and then some!
- In individual terms, it's aimed at
    - people who are happy to write but want to fine tune their skills
    - people who've never really thought about the fact they are in fact workplace writers, but now realise its importance and the diverse skills involved for self-growth and productivity
    - people who are nervous about writing for various reasons, and who need to develop confidence

The good news: it's a great leveller that we *all* need help in this fast-changing world. Our method will help all. What an opportunity this creates for us to take stock of our communication skills and keep up, not fall behind!

PART 2: The history – the written word was powerful from the start

From time immemorial, writing evolved as the language of commerce – for people to communicate with others, person to person, to keep track of things and for other specific outcomes. That remains crucial today, doesn't it? So let's look at the background to writing. It developed with scribes who were dedicated communicators, and really shouldn't we be looking at ourselves that way too?

Let's start this great new opportunity for a learning journey here. For example, as far back as 8000 BCE there's evidence of writing in cuneiform. In broad outline, it was devised:

- to extend the reach of spoken communication beyond the immediate interlocutors
- to provide a more permanent record of things discussed
- to consolidate systematic recording of things, such as trading transactions, laws, property, food distribution, in fact you name it, all the things we class as administration today

The earliest writers were educated and well-respected members of their communities. They welcomed intellectual growth and were prepared to put in the legwork (or should we say headspace!) on how to read and how to write.

But naturally, there's little point in recording things if we don't then:
- know what is meant
- ensure accuracy (and be prepared to verify)
- know how to act on what's recorded
- know how to disseminate this to the right people at the right time

And that's just for starters, as we'll be exploring in the book.

Interestingly, in Egypt the earliest and highly esteemed writers were known as scribes and 'tablet writers'. (Indeed we still use the word 'tablet' in today's parlance). Part of their prized professionalism was their expertise in passing on knowledge and contributing to the growing awareness that organised communities thrive.

Conversational writing came very much later, as did written poetry and literature.

Having looked at how business was the foundation stone for the earliest writing, let's fast forward to what's happening in our business communication today because the changes afoot are arguably second to none.

The fork in the road – where should we be going with our business writing today?

What *does it mean to us* when the world of business writing is turning on its head? The dawn of AI is one of the greatest changes in the world of business akin to the Industrial Revolution or the creation of the internet itself. It definitely means we avail ourselves of all the amazing help AI tools can offer, which we'll address in the book. But what it also means is that it's time to lean in to our greatest assets as humans:
- our personal and human uniqueness and personality
- our critical thinking skills and creativity
- our ability to engage and collaborate
- our ability to form and sustain relationships

And the differentiator for sustainable success will be to apply these to our business writing. We'll be helping you to just that throughout the book via the **which4words** method that provides the prompts *for you* to write successfully in each task, with the help of AI where appropriate, but with you still at the helm, writing as a human for humans.

Let's look at our starting point now

See how written messages have burgeoned – and how their nature has and is changing!

The number of written messages sent daily are truly staggering. Although hard to pinpoint an exact number, some references (Radicati Group, 2021) suggest globally some 376.4 billion emails are sent globally every single day – a number that is likely still growing. It's a huge number considering the global population stands at the time of publication, somewhere close to the 8.2 billion mark (Worldometer, 2025).

The nature of these digital communications has also dramatically changed, with the use of short form internet-based messaging being of great importance. As an example, in 2023 Meta reported 140 billion messages sent across WhatsApp, Messenger, and Instagram direct messages (DMs) every day (Meta, 2023).

Within the workplace, Microsoft reported in 2023 that the use of digital chat via their Teams platform increased from 13M daily active users in 2019 to 300M+ daily active users in 2023.

Interestingly, Microsoft also notes people now spend more time in Teams Chat, writing messages than in email (Microsoft, 2023).

In 2025 the rise of large language models, (LLMs), AI tools, mixed media tools such as AR/ XR to name but a few, make it clear this monumental change to the way we communicate will continue at a greater pace than ever before.

So where do we fit in, in this digital evolution?

The digital revolution or evolution we've experienced over the past decade or so, is quite staggering. One of the major changes is that the majority of businesses use AI for certain business writing tasks. Estimates are that it could be about 78% and even upwards to 90% (Exploding Topics, 2025; Digital Silk, 2025). This stat is unlikely to go down.

Also, with our access to personal computing devices, smartphones and so on, the widespread access to the internet has created what's often termed 'a democratisation of digital communication.' Why? Because now, when it's easier than ever before to fire off a text message, internet message, email, or anything in between, we're all empowered to have a voice. And we expect our voice to be heard.

When it comes to workplace writing, we expect open dialogue and inclusivity, involving the very real likelihood that our ideas matter when wider decisions are made, by management and others. Let's not forget we're all consumers too, and in that capacity we also expect businesses to treat our written messages seriously.

We increasingly appreciate that AI will come into the equation when it comes to processing information, but we still expect the overall communication experience to feel human to human, and that our values will feature. And just look at the vast area that business writing covers:

Reports/Recording information/Instruction and other manuals/Handbooks/PR/ Proposals and bids/Legal, Health and Technical documentation etc./Brochures/ Advertising/Newsletters/Formal letters/Social media/Customer service

AI is an important part of today's business writing – so how best to harness its help?

Yes, it's a great 'partner' helping businesses with routine and repetitive tasks such as drafting legal or other documents, templates, data analysis, SEO and certain aspects of marketing, HR, and healthcare to name a few. It also checks punctuation and grammar, in fact many of the so-called 'boring' bits of writing, freeing employees to focus on the more 'interesting' bits such as planning, strategy, creativity and authentic customer service.

The time AI can save us is a huge bonus. The way it can organise tasks for us, even kickstart us out of the writer's block some experience when facing the oh so many office writing tasks is fantastic. It's a springboard alright.

That said, people still need to carry out regular checks, because AI does make errors on many levels. We need to be mindful of this, and take remedial action where needed. And there are increasing signs of emergent kickbacks; of humans reclaiming their communication territory, so to speak, because of a myriad of challenges.

Part 3: Challenges you'll face in business writing today, whoever you are and whatever you do!

The written word isn't waning today but, at all levels, our grasp of it can be. Take a moment to think about that.

Are we lessening the communication interaction that writing was originally designed to do, when today it comprises so much inconsequential chat and noise, or so much *automated talking at people, rather than for them?*

Can we oftentimes be losing sight of how important business writing is, to all of us, no matter what stage of our career? And how we should be *actively* writing for positive outcomes? We'll be examining challenges we face which are often people-generated, as we'll be discussing throughout the book, and sometimes specifically AI generated, which we highlight next.

The sometimes big, sometimes small AI writing errors

Researching this book and preparing examples of do's and don'ts has opened many interesting doors – but one of the most interesting has to be the reflection on how AI or LLMs are actually working (or sometimes not working), and how this helps us realise just how vital our own written communication skills are. We could say they're more important than ever before.

Currently, it's fairly easy to tell when AI has generated something. There can be stylistic cues such as an often 'waffly' overcooked text littered with exotic words, that although correct, are not in common usage. That doesn't sit well with the prevailing view that plain language works best in business.

Intuition also comes into play: it's a human characteristic that AI can't share. As humans we can be empathetic and learn to recognise the tone or traits of the people we interact with. We can immediately tell when these are missing.

We'll be highlighting some of the bigger errors that AI can make later in the book, including *hallucinations* and *name disambiguation* for example, which can even lead to defamation cases (see Chapter 5). Things can go completely wrong, because of faulty inputting or even intrinsic engineering problems, or maybe AI tries to make sense of something but fails, lacking human intuition.

But right now let's take a look at some of the smaller errors that can often get through unnoticed. They shouldn't, because they are still meaningful: for example when AI generates images of people, hands may have 6 fingers instead of 5 . . . words may have random extra letters added on to the end. Or you may have seen something, perhaps in the middle of a block of text, for example, 'airpspace' instead of 'airspace,' or the order of a sentence, although correctly inputted, may become inexplicably jumbled.

Have you ever asked yourself why these little errors occur?
Without going into too much detail, large language models (LLMs) essentially scour the online world, reading and gathering data available. Words are then broken down into chunks or 'tokens' and, based on the task at hand, the model reassembles and uses logic to predict what the best output should be.

This is different to the way in which we recall language from childhood on, as we'll be exploring in Chapter 3, and apply it to convey our purpose/desire. The models also experience so called 'attention drift,' which leads to possible repetition or small errors, the longer a text may get.

Understanding this even at the most basic level, allows us to reflect on a number of important things to watch out for.

Quality of Inputs – errors in, errors out

Any large language model (LLM) output can only ever be as good as the inputs it receives to learn. Any model taught using texts full of grammatical or factual errors is likely to lead to poor output. The results can even be comical. For example, in a popular meme, when AI was asked to draw a map of Europe, the output was rife with mistakes, made up names and just generally incorrect (Cybernews, 2025). This was such a glaring error that people quickly noticed it and spread it online.

But if we don't check and keep highlighting how important it is for humans to focus on accuracy, more than ever before, can you see how the repercussions of not doing this could have bigger consequences than you ever imagined?

Words inadvertently or otherwise 'painted with the AI brush'

Although it's often easy to tell what AI has generated or not, the lines will continue to blur.

Software to identify what is real and what's not, is being more frequently deployed. Computers can be programmed to find and block such applications . . . but what are they looking for?

Well it can be to unearth scammers targeting people with ever more refined phishing attempts. We also see it used increasingly in areas such as academia, where professors and teachers find themselves plagued by AI generated exam submissions. An article in The Guardian newspaper in December 2024 went as far as calling this a crisis.

The article claims that more than half of all students use AI to support them during their assessments. It focuses on the ever escalating 'arms race' of trying to identify and then disqualify those thought to be cheating (Coldwell, 2024).

But there's a particularly bitter example of words inadvertently 'painted with the AI brush' where one student was hauled in front of a disciplinary panel, and threatened with disqualification, even though he protested he hadn't used the technology.

Why was that? Well there were many mistakes or 'signposts' consistent with the typical identifiers we've just mentioned around AI content. The student was embarrassed by, in effect, *being forced to apologise* for what was simply a badly written essay.

So what's the lesson here? It clearly underlines how important it is to be seen to get your written communications right yourself, from academia on. The student in question was in danger of being disqualified simply because his writing displayed the sort of characteristics and errors common in AI writing today.

Without any bad intentions, writing without purpose or making your own frequent small mistakes might accidentally see you on the wrong end of such 'filters'. You have been warned!

It's not just AI's communication we have to evaluate: it's our own!

Written communication skills can be on the decline, partly for reasons we'll be further discussing in Chapter 3, and partly to do with today's educational, digital, and technological landscapes.

Employers are flagging up that fewer students are exiting the education system with great writing skills. Why is this? Well, so many secondary school teachers are bemoaning the fact that current syllabuses (assigned to, not designed by them) come over as 'boring'. They need to be rehauled, to demonstrate that effective communication is based on:

- thinking (there's no substitute for this. It has to be the first step!)
- communicating logically, and creatively if necessary
- evaluating how well communication is working (checking how readers are reacting)
- enjoying writing, knowing it to be a lifelong skill worth developing

The building blocks need to be in place, and we pick up on this in Chapter 3.

Moving on to the next stage, studying English (and indeed other Arts and Humanities subjects) at university level, is losing out to what some may consider 'a better career option' in Science and Technology. Yet, traditionally in some cultures, businesses often recruited and relied upon Arts and Humanities graduates for their proven communication skills, seeing these as a valuable commodity.

Employers are now waking up to how they need to accommodate this changing scenario

The ability to express oneself, to convey a message to others, to convince, to sell, to connect, indeed, to communicate generally, all come within the remit of business writing. So why is its importance so often overlooked or taken for granted, as a basic skill that everyone has already mastered? They haven't. Because wherever we look:

- at the business minds of tomorrow in education today
- at people making their first steps in the business world
- all the way through to seasoned professionals
- and at those for whom writing can present particular challenges because of neurodiversity considerations such as dyslexia (which we'll cover shortly, as well as in Chapter 6)

most everyone in this list seems to be struggling to harness, elevate and indeed relish the effective use of the written word as the ultimate business tool. This in turn can create a negative spiral of reluctance, apprehension and even avoidance. This is bad for productivity, for customer service, for brand, for professionalism, for morale. The list continues. And yet whilst more words are being put on screen (and paper) than ever before, ironically less is often actually being said or done! We need the *right* words and the *right* outcomes.

The busy, attention deficit digital world, ironically made even more complicated by the rise of so-called AI tools, meant to help us, in effect make that busy world even busier!

And savvy businesses are taking more notice of their employees' writing skills, and what's the best way to help them develop them, according to role. Because skills will vary, people are individuals and that's the beauty of being human.

Employees' approach to business writing – what are we likely to find?

In broad outline, in organisations we're likely to find:

a) People who are confident they know the basics and more
Yes, of course they exist, although numbers may be dwindling. Not only is this cohort likely to have a good grasp of punctuation and grammar, but they're also likely to tune in to the importance of tone as well. Overall, they're not fazed by business writing and are likely to be the most proficient at writing prompts or queries for AI to interpret.

b) People who are disinterested in business writing
This might be because they've never really had to use it. At recruitment stage, employers may ask them to show one or two examples of emails they've written, as 'proof' that they have writing skills. Some employers settle for this minimum level of ability, in the belief that new entrants will learn further communication skills on the job. It might work, but it's not a given when workplace-wide, standards seem to be

slipping year by year, compounded by a world where training budgets for effective business writing have been slashed.

c) People who are actively nervous, even overwhelmed, at the thought of having to write on any level

They might hope that voice notes are where the business world is at and feel more comfortable with that. But voice notes yield problems of their own, often rambling, slipping into chat, taking up too much valuable time, not getting to the point or getting to a point that doesn't make sense without context! And they still do so often require written follow up to provide an audit trail.

This cohort's nervousness about the more permanent communication that writing can afford can stem from the fact they're having a tough time even figuring who they are, and what their voice is. We'll help with this in following chapters.

d) People with dyslexia – or other processing considerations

These can form a specific subset of c) and interestingly, the British Dyslexia Association suggest that roughly 10% of the UK population are dyslexic – a statistic that most likely translates to the workforce (British Dyslexia Association, 2025). Their approach can have so much to offer in this new landscape, when teachers and managers nurture their skills, as this case study shows.

CASE STUDY – Theo Paphitis, Chair at Theo Paphitis Retail Group and dyslexia champion

Charismatic retail magnate, Theo Paphitis, also finds time to foster a Small Business Sunday #SBS community with over 450,000 followers, as well as supporting the British Dyslexia Association as their first Dyslexia Empowerment Patron.

One of his posts on LinkedIn in this connection reads as follows:

"Dyslexia isn't a weakness. It's a different way of seeing the world.

It pushes you to find creative routes around the usual roadblocks and teaches you to see patterns others might miss. That kind of flexibility doesn't just build skills; it builds grit.

What really makes the difference is understanding. Teachers who adapt, friends who get it, workplaces that listen – all of that turns frustration into progress. Support that meets you where you are is what helps you thrive.

Dyslexia isn't about falling behind, it's about learning to move differently, and often, further than you thought you could." (Paphitis, 2025)

These wise words are likely to apply to other neurologically diverse ways of seeing the world, which teachers and managers need to make themselves aware of, and very importantly offer the support needed. In addition there are many accessibility guidelines out there, and compliance can be a legal requirement. We'll draw your attention to some of the leading ones that specifically pertain to business writing in Chapters 6 and 7.

There are always solutions, and you can imagine how enthused we are that our new **which4words** method is sure to be a major help to *all* these groups, and we know how *all* groups bring strengths to the table. We need to listen and learn and also see the advantage that a simple, beautifully flexible system like **which4words** can afford all.

Exercise

Which cohort do you most identify with? Or would you describe where you sit differently?

Whichever you most identify with, it's helpful to be aware of all these factors and seek hacks that help all round, as we have designed **which4words** *to do.*

An upside-down world: where we increasingly have to be all things to all people in our communication!

All these major shifts in the dial are also leading to what we could call an 'upside-down world' where we're almost all expected to have a vast communication toolkit – all too often without training. We increasingly find it's not just the dedicated marketing and internal communications specialists and the professional influencers who have to write as brand ambassadors and understand 'push' and 'pull' principles: it's all of us!

That's how important and far-reaching our written messages can be. We're all expected to be influencers now! If you're wondering what the principles of pull and push are, we'll give a brief summary here.

Push – a one-way communication where you initiate a message to send out (push) important company information, and you don't expect a reply. It helps productivity to state this. Everyone knows where they're at. Result.

Pull – a two-way communication where you respond to someone else's request. Maybe someone externally has been seeking information about your company. Internally, maybe someone is asking for something from you. You become the responder with the information they receive (pull) from you. And here you can often prevent overload by getting to the point quickly as far as possible, and in more complex cases you could consider providing a link to extra information – should that be what the person might also be looking for. It helps productivity and is naturally very helpful in customer service, for example.

Whether you use push or pull, or combine the strategies, the everyday writer won't have to work out detailed click rates as the specialists do. But you need to notice which of your messages gets read and which gets replied to. You need to try to work out why this is and adapt as necessary.

And as if this isn't challenging enough, you'll be noticing that a communication skillset that's especially prized, involves going further and knowing how to combine technical and creative writing in our daily tasks. That's a demanding new development too.

Suddenly specialist workers such as:

– technical/engineering/scientific/IT employees etc. now realise they need to add creativity to their writing skillset

– creatives now realise they need to add technical and IT skills to their communication toolkit

In fact we could go further to say that we're in a world where a winning communication skillset demands we *all* become technician, creative, marketer, influencer, and project manager.

If we ask who needs business writing skills, more to the point: who doesn't?

Whether you are working in a large organisation managing a team of people, or one of the people being managed, hoping to continue your development, chances are business writing is important in your daily life. The same applies whether you're working as a service provider or are a client directing work, or you're a volunteer or just organising a formal social event. Whether you're an administrator, or in fintech, law, HR or healthcare, or providing customer service, or writing computer code that will end up being read to thousands – the list is endless so, no matter what your application – yes, the chances are that you will write at work.

Treat it with the importance it deserves to get it right and let this book help you to improve.

Bosses also need to shout this out loudly and clearly! They know it matters – but they're not training staff sufficiently. Time to consider fresh solutions!

Part 4: Time to react to a great new opportunity: introducing the which4words approach

New solutions are needed on how best to plan and execute our business writing today. And the fact that we're living in an attention economy coupled with the rise of AI tools that can assist with our business writing tasks afforded us, the writers of this book, a Eureka moment!

For many years now, one of your authors has delivered management training courses based on her very well received 4-step writing system (which we use organically throughout the book and reveal in detail in Chapter 7, by which time you'll have seen how it works for yourselves!). This has helped individuals and teams at all levels of writing proficiency, in almost every type of business, understand how a well-defined, simply structured approach opens minds and delivers results.

Your other author has been reflecting on the practical themes in modern business and the overriding need for simplification in attention-deficit times. In fact his focus on simplifying communication to get the results needed, has been one of the greatest contributing factors to his extensive career success.

So we brought our two winning perspectives together, to bring something helpful for everyone, into an ultimate modern-day guide. And the notion of **which4words** sprang to our minds: a solution to kickstart effective writing that was just waiting to be unearthed!

Let's make sure we keep control of the 'best bits' – the exciting bits of communication. The 'people' aspects, the creative aspects, the logic to come up with strategy and know-how to think about how to achieve successful outcomes, verification (yes, that's key too) – and understanding what we want from our communication (our Purpose and Compass, our objectives etc.) and what others need from us, all of which we'll cover in the book.

That's an impressive to-do list, isn't it? Then what if, to help us achieve all this:
- we had a system whereby we asked ourselves the right questions, designed to boost our business writing success?
- we used this system to break concepts down into individual powerful words, to communicate clearly and succinctly in the modern world
- we used those words, our personalised prompts in effect, just for us, as a springboard that dynamized our ensuing communication

Wouldn't it be helpful?

The which4words approach at your service

So we've created a new system, and we can't wait to share how it works with you. In a world where a winning communication skillset demands you become technician, creative, marketer, influencer, and project manager, the **which4words** method provides ground-breaking prompts that give guidance for every writing task.

We'll show you how to tailor these prompts not for AI but for YOU and your communication needs, by:

1. Encouraging you to retain, harness and indeed celebrate the human touch that's so vital in writing tasks
2. Helping you get to the point swiftly and effectively for maximum impact
3. Providing the tools to cut through the noise and stand out in an increasingly digital age
4. As a result, armed with confidence and enthusiasm, being the best communicator you can be

We could identify **which4words** as the prompts in bold type below. to summarise these four points as:

1. **Encouragement** – (to celebrate human touch)
2. **Impact** – (get to the point, in the right way)
3. **Tools** – (know how to do it)
4. **Best** – (that's how you want to be seen)

*Note: The descriptive words we have just used (in brackets) are intended as a memory aid. What's key is that you identify the 4 words that best describe your **which4words** in each task, and briefly add notes in brackets, if that helps further.*

Ways to apply the which4words method to your business writing

Here are some of the principal ways in which you can apply the **which4words** approach to your business writing. More will emerge as you work your way through all the examples we'll illustrate in each chapter. Through reinforcement, the system will be second nature to you by the end of the book:

1 As a planning tool
This ensures you know:
–   what you're trying to communicate
–   what you would like your readers/audience to take away from your message

This helps you to quickly structure your writing to get to that defined, and now well laid out point. To benefit from this application, you would typically curate/personalise these four words up front, before you begin a writing task. Once you've written something, then check back that you've achieved your **which4words** objectives for the reader before you send!

Let's say, for example, you're chasing a critical update for a project deadline that is approaching a critical milestone. Feedback has been poor, and you are seeking reassurance that everything is on track. You understand, however, that the team is feeling the pressure of the deadline, so you want and need to appear supportive.

In this scenario your **which4words** might be:

1. **Status**
2. **Urgency**
3. **Dialogue**
4. **Support**

By using this simple hack, you'll find yourself writing in a more effective and efficient way. It allows us to quickly target our desired outcome and have a reference point to check back on to make sure our writing says what we intended.

Likewise let's imagine you're tasked with writing a monthly report. This might include many standard slides/information that's always required – but this month you additionally need to chase a specific approval for a budget increase. Your **which4words** might be:

1. **Context**
2. **Change**
3. **Discussion**
4. **Approval**

Looking back after finishing your presentation or report, you should then ask: does the document nicely facilitate this desired set of focus areas? Again, a simple but effective roadmap to keep your writing on track and your audience crystal clear on what you are trying to say/achieve.

2 As a tool to help you write for humans

This has other wide-reaching and exciting benefits. For example, think of an interaction with an employee who may have made a mistake or is struggling with performance issues and might need some coaching or guidance. This is likely to be a difficult, possibly even emotional conversation, so preparing with an email setting the scene could significantly help to set the tone.

The **which4words** you might curate, personalised to your task, could be:

1. **Constructive**
2. **Candid**
3. **Development**
4. **Growth**

Can you see that when we just launch into writing, or even worse, don't think at all and fire off a one liner, we tend to create misunderstanding, wrong or missing connections, and attendant doubt. None of these factors help either party.

On the other hand using the **which4words** method to plan out quickly/roughly what you actually want to convey and achieve can be a simple superpower.

3 As a useful tool for calibration/summarising

We all have a lot of written communication coming our way. Modern digital tools such as AI are picking up the slack, summarising texts for us and trying to make our lives more manageable. But as we'll be referring to throughout, reading, understanding, focusing is the add on we need to provide. This is key to successful interaction and true communication.

Do get in the habit of calibrating others' written messages to you as well as yours to them. By this we mean observing and interpreting where others are coming from as well as the actual message they send. It can mean reading between the lines and then summarising your findings. Check your own understanding and play it back to others if necessary.

Now let's say you've received a long project report on the monthly status of a project and yes, you understand that everything's on track. You want to congratulate the team and reinforce that, should there be any issue at all, your door is always open. The **which4words** prompts you curate for yourself could be:
1. **Celebrate**
2. **Reinforce**
3. **Listen**
4. **Support**

On the other hand, you might have read the report and noticed a risk that you feel is not being given the proper level of cross-functional attention and could quickly become a showstopper if not well-managed. Then your **which4words** might be:
1. **Highlight**
2. **Escalate**
3. **Remove**
4. **Status**

See how flexible the method is – it's for you to curate and personalise

So **which4 words** would you choose in the same situation?

There's no right or wrong, simply whatever works for you. But whether writing an immediate reply, preparing ongoing reports, thinking up campaigns, discussions with colleagues etc. – or simply capturing your thoughts for your own follow-up, this can be such a help in your everyday business life!

Indeed we can also look at countless examples from the world of customer service to further underline how this simple daily hack of summarising information we receive, can lead to totally different outputs.

Let's look at one instance right now.

CASE STUDY – Missing the point is rife

Having recently required a replacement oven shelf for an older model oven, Ralf contacted a specialist supplier who advertised that they stocked these parts.

Their website stated loud and proud – we pride ourselves in the human touch – contact us today – our specialists have the expert knowledge to help!

So Ralf fired off his email asking for that help:

Hi there!

I am looking for a replacement oven shelf for my oven. I sadly do not know the model number as the sticker with the information has worn away, and as it's fully integrated, I can't look behind the machine. I have included photos of the oven, dimensions of the tray and, as it was purchased in 2016, I have narrowed it down to either Model X or Model Y.

Hope you can help!

Many thanks in advance,

Kind regards,

Ralf X

After one week, the reply came:

Dear Mr. X,

Thanks for reaching out to us! We would be glad to help.

Please kindly send me your oven model number. This is usually located on a sticker around the opening of the oven – alternatively on the side or back of the unit.

We look forward to helping you find the part you need.

Yours,

Customer Service

Looking at the request, and the answer – what comes to mind first? Auto-text? Or simply the company had not read the request properly?

The sad fact is that such responses that totally miss the point are becoming rife. They frustrate customers, and in the worst-case lead to loss of customers/customer satisfaction.

At the very least, these responses are inefficient simply because they lead to more back and forth communication between both parties, with a complete lack of focus by the companies concerned that customers ultimately pay their wages!

How might we have summarised the initial request and our intended reply in **which4words**? Perhaps:

1. **Reassurance** – (Empathising with the customer: this happens all the time – they have come to the right place)
2. **Questioning** – (perhaps interrogating further to get to the missing information. Maybe there'll be an instruction manual? Confirming a full understanding of the problem)
3. **Research** – (Outlining next steps – perhaps a list of potential models – and the time this might require)
4. **Proposal** – (managing expectations on potential cost/likelihood of finding an exact match etc.)

Your journey starts here: identify where things are at, and where you need to be

Let's start this new journey, systematically: the best way to work. Figure out what you need to do to achieve the best business writing you can.

When to push ahead with AI versus when to push back for the human touch

The debate is definitely on, not just in the academic world that we looked at earlier.

Take a quick look at any social media business forums and you'll see people increasingly reacting to the unquestioned, unverified use of AI in business writing.

Of course it has fans – as we've already listed, so many of its applications are great. But you'll also find a growing number of people who feel there needs to be a partial push back at the very least. Complaints abound that AI eclipses the human touch and that written communication has too many important 'strings to the bow,' to ever be 'outsourced' to AI.

The stakes are too high they argue, citing the slur 'clanker,' to refer to the situation as they see it. The term originated in the Star Wars franchise but in today's business parlance, it's used to cover growing scepticism about an over reliance on automation (covering robots and LLMs etc.) and the societal repercussions. Sceptics want to see people regain their 'rightful' place, not superseded by machines. They are passionate about delivering communication that keeps humans centre stage which clearly doesn't when it's:

- formulaic programming
- unimaginative and
- unengaging

Feelings run strong on this topic. It's time to ask you your thoughts on this. Do ask colleagues too – and why not write your findings down here? We'll be examining this topic in more detail in Chapter 5.

What the power of the written word means to you

What you've read so far will be giving you a new perspective, so let's capitalise on this now.

Exercise

Take a moment to answer these questions.

1. *How do you feel about business writing generally ?*
2. *What are your strengths?*
3. *What fazes you?*
4. *How would you like to feel?*

We're aiming to get you to point 4 by the end of this book!

Use this new perspective to drive your success

Our toolkit to help you is fully thought through on many levels, so that you profit from this new perspective by:

1. Summing things up in a way that suits you and what you need to do, based on the **which4words** method
2. Leaving you centre stage, where you need to be, personalising the key prompts, chapter by chapter

3.   Building your own tailored Word Bank, so to speak, that you can choose to borrow from and make transfers to, as you go along. Whatever you do you'll profit at each business writing task
4.   Letting AI do the heavy lifting on the perimeter, as we'll explain as we go

Refocus and adjust your mindset: put YOURSELF at the forefront of the AI age

Allow yourself that important breathing space and refocus. You'll amass great career benefits. Take a long, hard, much-needed look at a world where written business communication can be, how shall we say, a bit fuzzy? A bit discombobulated? What might you add?

Identify the challenges as you see them – then source the solutions
The scribes of ancient times knew exactly why they were writing. Nowadays we can hardly argue that there's progress when we routinely find that:
–   People don't necessarily understand the full purpose of why they're communicating
–   They don't listen
–   They don't enquire
–   They don't enjoy reading and only skim read – not understanding that effective writing so often results from attentive reading
–   They don't focus on meaning or what really needs to happen next
–   They don't understand how to organise their thoughts into writing that works
–   They don't care
–   They are overwhelmed

Only when you first address the challenges you know you have, can you address them – and solve them! And they'll be different for everyone. For some it will be:
–   How to get to the point efficiently, and make more use of simple words and phrases
–   How to avoid making mistakes, understanding the physical cost of putting things right as well as the cost to reputation
–   How to adapt language (personal v professional and according to target audience and channel)
–   How to systematically communicate quality, values, and aspiration
–   How to influence
–   How to communicate well and connect in teams (mindful too of culture/diversity/neurodiversity)

- How to communicate and connect with customers, understanding their needs too
- Why are my messages often ignored (even 'ghosted' in today's parlance) so often?
- When people do respond, it's not always for the right reason. Why is that?

We all still need to know how to communicate ourselves don't we?

The communication equation was ever thus:

Accurate and well-thought-through input in, the right results out

Empowering: You're in control in this book

Unearth *the essence of you as an individual*. We'll always retain our creative advantage as humans, but what we are in danger of, is losing sight of it!

This book will put you firmly in control of your written communication. All the concepts you summarise in powerful words to get to the point, in effect the prompts we'll help you identify and personalise, will be about YOU. They'll place you in the foreground of the tasks you face, and the interaction you need with your world of work (and the added bonus is that it's likely to help your social life too).

Robots can be our valuable virtual assistants, but they don't replace us and they're not our colleagues.

All the power of the written word comes from YOU

- You are providing the toolkit
- You are learning how best to connect with individuals, with wider audiences and potentially engaging with the world
- You are understanding your ability to influence
- Where you want your place to be in the world is in your hands
- You'll appreciate how efficient communication comes in a variety of ways!

which4words in summary

As this first chapter draws to a close, why not use **which4words** to summarise your takeaways? Let's get into the habit of using the method as we go. As we see it, we could use these words (with a short explanation in brackets following each):

1. **Context** – (how the world of business writing is changing around us)
2. **Action** – (the time to adapt our communication is now)
3. **System** – (a simple way of approaching writing)
4. **You** – (are the centre of your success)

Why not also create a Word Bank to summarise this and each ensuing chapter?

Because we are so passionate about word power to spur your communication to success, you don't have to stop there. Why not consider building your own relevant Word Bank at the end of each chapter? This will be a useful exercise to help you break down concepts into individual powerful words as an important step on your journey to successful communication.

In time you'll build up your own comprehensive Word Bank, from which you can borrow, make transfers, and build up multiple groupings of **which4words** to suit every scenario you encounter. It's something you can definitely profit from throughout every twist and turn in your career.

For this chapter we could suggest a Word Bank as follows:

WORD BANK

Realise   Learn   Adapt   Communicate   Opportunity   Transformative   Personalise   Yes!   Self-growth   Connection   Influence   Clarity   Professionalism   Career-skills   Awareness   Curiosity   Success   Productive   Efficient   Problem-solving   Enthusiasm   Ambition   AI   Confidence   Trust   Impactful   Interest   Systematic   Perspective   Creative   Technical   Aspiration   Vital   Commitment   Consistent   Empowerment   Control   Focus   Unfazed   Confidence   Fundamentals   Basics   Human   Personal   Voice   Celebrate   Reinforce   Support   Question   Confirm

---

2 Why everyone's business writing matters

This chapter reaffirms how business writing is our main interface with the new world and, whether digital or analogue, it needs to work.

In outline, let's focus on:
- Why it matters to get it right, on many levels
- What a wide-ranging subject it is – in which to maintain your voice *consistently*
- Which **which4words** prompts will you choose, to kickstart you to results in the task in hand?

The communication formula to keep in mind every time!

Written communication will only be effective if we're systematic. We first need to identify in our minds the right message for the task in hand, then convert it into the right writing, then choose the right medium to send the message to the right people at the right time in the right way for us and for them, (at the same time realising that the message might be forwarded to people we didn't expect it to be as can be the way in the digital world), and then we need to check the message worked in the way we intended.

All of this explains *why* we need to get all aspects of our business writing to work, not just to get results but to meet all attendant expectations and showcase our values and professionalism.

It's hardly a soft option, but throughout we're going to give you the toolkit that makes it so much easier to navigate!

which4words 'sense check'

You'll see throughout the book that we'll be using the system in various scenarios. You will soon become adept in using it. To set you on course, and in the spirit of being clear about what you are trying to say, we'll set out an initial 'sense check' in this chapter. Our intention here, at our planning stage, is that you will leave it thinking about the following concepts:

1. **Pitfalls** – (how 'little' mistakes can have big consequences)
2. **Efficiency** – (how you and your communication directly impact productivity)
3. **Impact** – (how your communication can affect others)

© 2026 Walter de Gruyter GmbH, Berlin | https://doi.org/10.1515/9783112217696-003

4. **Planning** – (how planning how and what you write can unlock limitless success)

Don't let 'busyness' take our eye off the goal!

You just have to look in any office to see people madly clacking away at keyboards – but are they really achieving the results they should be? Messages that work? If you analyse *results* it soon becomes clear that *'busyness'* isn't necessarily linked to productivity.

Good intentions gone bad: Communication tools used wrongly

It's clear that the tools and methods around to try to help us improve our communication don't always do that. They can be used incorrectly if we, as humans, don't think for ourselves why it matters to get our writing right. And things can actually get worse as we'll show.

Knowledge Management always made easy?

There are currently a raft of automated knowledge or project management tools available in the workplace. Providers do great elevator pitches as to why you should use them, expressed chiefly and simply (and guess what, we can summarise the usual pitch in 4 steps!):
1. Replace outdated emails or legacy office solutions
2. Organise your projects in simple to use centralised repositories
3. Empower your employees. Allow them to organise themselves!
4. Unlock the unharnessed potential of your workforce!

And yes, the pitch usually continues, you can try it for free. Sign me up, you may think!

On the surface it can sound like a dream. No more overloaded inbox. Your own dashboard with all critical tasks perfectly laid out and prioritised. The ability to link to your targets, the resourcing of your team. Etc. etc.

But user training can be sketchy once the software's in place, and then what do we so often see? Many people soon ending up having to default back to their old emails, and of course face-to face communication, for one simple reason: *the use of the system itself became the goal.*

The '*Why am I communicating?*' can be lost! Instead we have countless examples of people 'looking busy' by spending the bulk of their time creating and completing tasks.

Task duplication soon becomes rife when everyone's empowered to *create* but few zone into the bigger picture that they also need to *curate* messages that work. This is a key message in this book where **which4words** will emerge as your unique curation tool, personalised by you, to deal with the 'why am I writing, what do I want to achieve, and how do I do it successfully in each writing task?'

Because if we don't curate, what happens? Information overload! Confusion! Frustration! People so often discovering that the pitched 'free trial' of the latest communication software can soon turn into something that users pay dearly for, in every sense of the word! 'THE HOW' can eclipse 'THE WHY' around business writing, and that doesn't make commercial sense at all.

Some hard facts on why it matters to get writing right

Here are some hard facts that demonstrate that business writing should never be considered to be a soft option although, strangely, it's so often labelled as a soft skill!

a) Business writing affects objectives and the bottom line

We'll look into these aspects more fully in ensuing chapters – but let's start off with an outline of what business writing's objectives might be:
- They might be informational, or instructional
- They might be to attract and engage for transactional reasons, e.g. sales
- They might be to raise awareness of brand and values
- They might be to recruit, or
- To foster team collaboration
- They might be to sound opinions out and agree a way forward, or
- To look at how to solve problems or defuse an escalating situation
- They might be to persuade or to influence, or to motivate
- They might be to give people the feelgood factor (and how often do we ignore the opportunity to do that?)
- They might be to spread common values for social good and build communities

What a lot of possibilities ! And we haven't finished there; there'll be other objectives you'll think of – and that's the purpose of this book. It's to involve you; for you to come up with the **which4words** prompts that highlight the key points that will assist you to take each objective to success.

Because if you don't achieve your objectives as efficiently as you can, whatever they are, it's going to cost you on many levels.

These might be:

- lost business through missing your targets
- lost profits because muddled messaging led to the wrong outcomes (or no outcomes)
- extra costs incurred by not getting to the point/unnecessary iteration/need for clarification/duplication of work (more on this shortly)
- lost business because of something as simple as a typo

We'll just pick up on this one, as too many people say: 'Well to make typos is human, isn't it?' as if acceptance makes it alright.

Well for a start, lawyers, scientists, and healthcare professionals wouldn't agree, would they? In fact, should anyone? Typos can make readers feel that the writer is unprofessional, whether we like it or not. And of course typos can have real, material consequences across the board. Let's look at two recent examples.

BBC News reported that four tonnes of oysters caught by a Jersey shellfish exporter, the Jersey Oyster Company, and worth £11,000, were rejected at the French border due to an 'admin error' (Thomas, 2025). The error was just one typo in a reference number. You see that's business writing too. The reference number wasn't a legal requirement countered the owner of the Oyster Company, but the French authorities held firm: traceability mattered – and you can see their point when it comes to consumables.

That cost of £11,000 for a typo is a large amount for a small to medium player to pay.

And 'simple' typo errors can even cost far, far more. The BBC also reported on an error made by Bristol City Council when sending out council tax bills to residents where they had mistakenly shown that The Police Commissioner for Avon and Somerset had had a 5.9% rise, and the Avon Fire Authority quoted as 5%. The figures should have been the other way round. The Council referred to this as 'a typing mistake' and, in response to a written question as to how much it cost to send corrected letters out to residents, said it was £198,000 (Miller, 2025).

It shows how large financial costs can accrue from the slightest writing error. And even what you may consider the slightest error, such as writing a client's name wrongly, isn't slight to them. It can certainly lose goodwill, if not custom, which will of course affect profits too.

Yes, both the smaller and the larger errors matter. All communication needs to hit the mark as the reader expected.

That said, there's an interesting point to consider regarding *intentionally making mistakes.* This can be a viral campaign tactic which we'll address in Chapter 8!

b) It affects productivity

This can be in a number of ways, and we'll touch on some of the principal ones here.

Email and distraction overload

According to runn.io, office workers spend around 2.5 hours per day on email related tasks – clearly a considerable portion of the average working day. On top of this, their research suggests that workers check their emails roughly 11 times per hour (Runn, 2024)!

Not only does this lead into distraction (a point we will go into shortly), but it suggests at least partial pre-occupation with what might come into an email inbox – or potentially even the fear of missing something. Take note of the many tips we make in this book about making email more effective as a written tool and you'll find your readers will thank you. You'll thank yourself too.

Task switching and digital interruption

Scientists and psychologists are looking into the effects of these constant distractions in the field of 'interruption science.' Indeed Gloria Mark conducted a study of office workers where she observed office workers often only spend 11 minutes on a single task before being distracted. It's true that some distractions can be positive. If you're anxiously awaiting the latest sales figure before presenting to the board, that ping that brings you the numbers is really welcome. But so many pings are anything but, especially if they aren't to the point (Mark et al., 2005).

According to the same study, once a person is distracted, apparently it can take them around 25 minutes to re-focus on the original task.

Multiply this across a day or a week and you can see that the implications for productivity are profound.

Everything we can do to be clear, concise, and targeted with our communication, to reduce their overall volume, will reap great rewards when it comes to overall productivity.

What does this mean to you? The most important person in this book

We've discussed some of the statistics around productivity and effective business writing. Let's bring your experience into the picture.

You know for yourself that productivity takes a hit every time someone:

- has to ask the sender what the written message they received actually means
- has to ask for the question(s) they asked to be fully answered, not just partially
- has to point out mistakes that need correction
- escalates the written message they received into a complaint
- waffles on and doesn't get to the point, wasting your precious time
- misses the point because they haven't clarified what was needed before they sent the message
- ignores/ghosts you/doesn't reply as requested

The list could continue . . .

All of this contributes to unnecessary extra work that follows on if we want to achieve our objectives, that is. And if we don't – well even that's a huge hit on productivity!

We'll naturally be diving deeper into this, with examples, throughout the book. We'll be picking up on the effect of overload on productivity and time-wasting 'workslop' – which can be an unwanted feature of AI generated writing.

Just to elaborate, 'workslop' (Niederhoffer et al., 2025) is a word to describe low-quality, AI-generated work that appears polished but lacks substance, context, and accuracy. Research from BetterUp Labs and the Stanford Social Media Lab found that this phenomenon hinders productivity rather than helping it as it can noticeably shift the work from the producer (the writer) to the receiver, who has to spend time and effort:

- Understanding what is meant
- Checking and reworking as necessary
- Producing a professional, finished product – which is what business writing should be

Maybe 'a no-frills business writing checker' could help us all here! Very simply, the minute you find yourself slipping into a *check . . . correct . . . check . . . correct . . . check . . . correct seemingly endless loop* is likely to be the minute you're noticing 'workslop' if AI generated, or 'sloppywork' if human generated!

Exercise

*Here's an exercise for you to try out **which4words** for yourself.*

*Take a moment to think about the last long back and forth written exchange you had with someone in a business context. Something that may have been a misunderstanding, disagreement or simply felt like it took too long to settle. Take a look with fresh eyes and summarise the exchange using **which4words.***

What did you notice? Did any of the following appear?

1. **Confusion** – one of the parties was unclear as to what was required of them
2. **Lengthy** – a lot of messages were sent back and forth
3. **Frustration** – emotions began to run high
4. **Compromise** – was required to break the stalemate

If any of these resonate, go back and re-do the exercise from a planning point of view.

which4words might you have written down prior to approaching the situation?

To get writing right, it can help to address what gets it wrong!

It's always illuminating to pick up some vox pop: people randomly expressing what matters to them. Heartfelt thoughts spill out as to what writing irks them, way before they express what they like!

In fact when we announced to friends, family, and academic and business associates, that we were writing this book, nobody said 'Oh great! You're sure to mention what effective writing looks like.' No! What they did do, to a person, was to encourage and thank us, asking us to highlight *all the things that annoy them in business writing today!*

So what were the sorts of bugbears that commonly came up?

Here they are, set out in the conversational style people used:

"However busy someone is, don't I as the recipient deserve high standards from the writer? Poorly written, misspelt email, or messily constructed messages immediately tells me that quality doesn't matter and speaks volumes about their business"

"I get so annoyed when people write my name wrongly"

"My biggest bugbear is when my messages are ignored."

"Why don't people read what I've sent, think and answer all my questions
systematically?"
"I feel frustrated and undermined when my manager automatically accepts AI advice
over mine"
"Please, oh please, let a webchat be with a person!"
"Please write about the so annoying '5 Pings syndrome'!"
"Do mention how writing needs to be respectful!"
"Message threads are bad news if context's lost!"
"I'm drowning in overload! Please urge people to get to the point."

This authentic vox pop tells us, even more directly than any textbook, why it matters
to get writing right! What would you add? Do discuss this with others, and make a
note here:

We'll be systematically dealing with how to address all the points raised in subsequent chapters. But we'll address the 'Five Pings Syndrome' right now!

'The Five Pings' Poor Communication syndrome!

Picture this. It won't be hard to do. You're working in your office. And then ping,
ping, ping, ping, and ping in quick succession because some people hit send after
every line or sentence. It's the sound of your smartphone, and it's on fire!

How do you feel? Do you accept it as a totally normal situation? If so, should you?

How often can it be classed as effective writing? And if it is, then why are people
complaining about it? We think it can be for twofold reasons:

a) Operational

The pings might well have interrupted whatever you were doing and this chimes
with what we've been saying about business writing and productivity. True, you
could have pre-arranged with the sender to ping an urgent update on something as
soon as they knew it. That's fine.

But even then, is the five ping syndrome going to be the most productive?

Thinking about it, it could be the first ping that gets your attention. There's a
phenomenon known as the primacy effect, where our attention focuses more on the
first piece of information we receive in any chain. But it could also be the end message that we switch our main focus to. Or even the middle one, if that's the easiest
to process.

Time and time again, we're finding that readers don't afford the same level of
focus on each ping in a cluster of pings! Selective reading can come into play.

And what's the regrettable outcome? Inefficiency. The big picture will be lost, and that makes for very poor communication and very bad business outcomes.

And this lack of attention to the full picture spills over into general business writing. If we deal with matters in a piecemeal fashion, it's easy to fall into delivering piecemeal solutions. The upshot can be that situations, including problems, are:

– never fully dealt with
– or take longer to deal with, involving ever more pings, added to dollops of frustration/annoyance depending on who's involved!

b) Relational

The first ping might well have the connection line, maybe on the lines:

'Hope this finds you well' – and then the message carries on.

People who favour relational communication will look for this as their primary connection point. And if you break up the message in those further four pings, you can, without ever realising, disconnect the relationship, instead of building on it and creating further rapport. And rapport can help get people on side and enable successful outcomes.

This may not be your default style – but as it matters to so many, do be aware of it. We'll be examining this more in Chapter 6.

Not setting a baseline can hamper goals/reference/targets/briefs

So now let's look at another aspect where businesses create problems by ignoring why writing matters. It's this: (and follows on from our introduction to the written word in Chapter 1) effective business writing *shapes* projects and then becomes instrumental in delivering them.

A written brief can help – so think carefully before ditching them

We'll just take an incursion here into two separate business areas:

1. Marketing specifically
2. Project management generally

We've chosen these as they are areas where a written brief used to be the expected springboard from which everything panned out. But now that people are losing their grasp of the power of the written word, bosses increasingly lament the fact that written briefs increasingly seem to be on the way out.

Time to redress the balance we feel, and here's why. The power of the written word used to be front, centre and back of projects and marketing campaigns for a very good reason. Discount its value and it's literally a shock to any systemic approach to actively progress projects. This case study will show what we mean.

CASE STUDY – A Tale from the Coal Face: The Marketer's Take

Marcus owns and runs a successful international marketing agency. He laments the fact that some of what used to be seen as business *basics* seem to be falling by the wayside.

In his experience, as many as 80% of clients now fail to formally provide a written brief at the start of a commission or paid piece of work. Briefing meetings take place either face to face or via online platforms. Minutes are taken and circulated.

Channelling his inner project manager, Marcus knows *he now has to take on an extra step* to ensure likelihood of a positive outcome on any task or project. He believes in the power of a recorded written brief. If it's not there, intuitively his way of moving forward is by writing it himself. He now sets about achieving this by:

- Conferring with his client, after which *he* now has to write down a short summary of the brief
- He then gets his client to approve it
- Next he agrees with them on 4 metrics to judge the project's success

This way they arrive together at a working brief which keeps all on track – which, for example, could be to deliver an uplift in:

1. **Awareness**
2. **Differentiation**
3. **Meaning**
4. **Specifics** (project specific)

And hey presto, in points 1–4 we have yet another example of how **which4words** can present so easily as the kickstart prompts to success. You just have to look out for them and nurture them!

Setting the baseline – and over to you now

What's your business or area of expertise? How could you tailor the **which4words** method for your needs?

For example, on a commercial project the goal, the why it matters to get writing right, could be uplift in:

1. **Market-Share**
2. **Penetration** (New Users)
3. **Profit**
4. **Specifics** (Project Specific)

In the world of more general project management it could be:

1. **Plan**
2. **Source**
3. **Make**
4. **Deliver**

The message is simple: if you expect an output *then write down what it should look like,* or you'll simply spend your time turning in circles and/or being totally frustrated.

And if we again turn to 'The Marketer's Take' a strong written brief, agreed by both, can ensure the client doesn't waste time and money and, just as importantly for the agency, that they get the commission, and both are on the joint path to get results!

In all cases, the chances of success are slim to none if you're not clear on *and don't express* the expected output. That's why writing matters. A well thought-through written brief sent to the right people is:

– literally there for all to see
– unambiguously highlights what's involved
– a major factor in helping keep people on track

Business writing isn't just about 'mechanics': it's also about getting mindsets right!

We have to shape the communication landscape too – not just let the digital changes wash over us, with our guard down, sleepwalking on occasion into outcomes we didn't anticipate or want.

It's not enough to keep abreast, we need to keep ahead. Make suggestions, innovate. Want to be that reliable person, proud to be accountable for a job well done, and developing career prospects that you've worked on, that you've invested in. Ideally be that person that's consummately professional and proud to make their mark.

If your answer is yes you want to be that person, we're here at your service, to help you throughout the book.

Everything we suggest will be about trying to outline the way forward to effective business writing in **which4words** bite-sized steps.

Yes, let AI do the heavy lifting: we'll repeat this throughout, because it is an unstoppable force and has to feature in every chapter. Embrace the help it affords us in most of our writing tasks to plan, edit, scope, implement and so on, but never lose sight of your need to be at the helm.

Develop your communication toolkit at every turn. It actually starts from childhood on, as we'll demonstrate in the next chapter.

What would your Word Bank to summarise this chapter be?

Remember our suggestion in Chapter 1?
For this chapter we could suggest a Word Bank as follows:

WORD BANK

Universal Accessible Structured Systematic Focused Bugbears Distraction Curated Efficient Productive Effective Amicable Empathetic Focus Respectful Purposeful Considered Mindful Practical Baseline Innovate

---

What might your Word Bank for this chapter be?

3 Looking at when communication starts

You may be wondering why, in a book about business writing, we're keen to help you reconnect with your childhood communication phase. Read on to find out why.

In this chapter it all becomes very clear if:
- We look at communication through the eyes of a child and go back to basics
- The founding blocks of communication matter! Without them, how can our subsequent communication work optimally?
- There's increased understanding that today's business writing needs to create interest and engage, more than ever. Storytelling can be one tool that does just that. Don't just relegate imagination to your childhood phase!
- In parallel, we look at the effect of digitalisation right from the start and see its impact on communication in a time-pressured, low attention world
- This chapter helps you see the principles of effective communication are on a continuous sequence, that you should seek to grow, not discard, in each phase

---

When we're immersed in a world of short attention spans, and finding so many of our written (and spoken) messages ignored, or wrongly answered or other inefficiencies that arise, we need to ask ourselves: *'What's going on?'*

On one level, overload contributes to these problems – and in no small measure this is due to digitalisation. But aren't we also too often failing to take a step back . . . and reconnect with our childhood communication?

Of course there are understandable exceptions to take into account, but by and large, we didn't feel overwhelmed then, did we? So why was that? What's changed now?

Let's take a look at the phase now. Have you ever thought about it? In a nutshell, within the remit of this book, your childhood communication experience will have played a role in developing you as an individual as well as a social being.

Take a moment to remember how the world looked through your eyes as a child, how you persevered as far as you could in learning to read and write, how you interacted with the world, how your imagination ran riot, how your creativity flourished.

We can be in danger of forgetting these fundamental basics. Don't! If you have, well here's the opportunity to reframe your stance now, in adulthood. It will really sharpen your business writing skills today!

© 2026 Walter de Gruyter GmbH, Berlin | https://doi.org/10.1515/9783112217696-004

We become communication powerhouses from infancy on

Ever thought of putting it that way? It's something to celebrate: what an achievement – that you probably didn't even notice.

Language acquisition is the magical prime factor in how we interact with the world, right from the start. It helps us learn how to make connections with the most important people in our lives. The ones around us, the ones who cared for us.

We quickly expand the phase and our vocabulary to cover growing experiences, as we learn more about how the world works. We also draw on our imagination, hopefully seen through the lens of wonderment and enjoyment.

Don't lose this initial childhood joy – and ease in communication

Take a minute to step back into these early memories if you can. Close your eyes, take a deep breath and allow yourself a moment. What are the first words that jump into your head to describe these memories? They're worth recording, for future reference.

Interestingly, before you could read, you'll have looked at pictures and most likely spoken about them. Were you eager to turn a page over onto the next, to see what happened next?

What words and images spring to mind?

Successful writers or illustrators know how to stand out. To grab your attention.

Now go a step further. Which were *the positive* images and words? Which were more *negative*. Which would you prefer to take forward into your future life? Yes, the seeds start here! So which were the books you ditched fast? The boring ones, do we hear you say? And which did you avoid, given the choice, because maybe you didn't even like the look of them?

Now, just for a moment, fast forward to your future adult world and, for the purposes of this book, specifically to the world of work. Something's happening. Something rather negative is happening, creeping in, unchallenged. Rather too many people are describing school, college, and workplace communication as 'boring'.

How sad that this can happen when we lose focus on the childhood communication skills that can come so easily, so naturally:

- on the joy in listening
- on interacting positively
- on wanting to be read to, and then reading ourselves
- on being open to new ideas and discovering ourselves
- on creativity

– and even subliminally, seeing there's a structure in communication, however fluid

Regarding the last point, yes, children are drawn to the 'beginning, middle and end' structure of traditional storytelling, but they're also keen fans of the magic of open form poetry, and so on.

Allow ourselves to lose our curiosity and what happens? 'Boring' happens. It so easily becomes the norm we accept; our expectation, dare we say, our indoctrination! Let's throw that out, right here, right now.

Maybe we can now summarise your initial communication phase into the first of our **which4words** suggestions (in no particular order):

1. **Curiosity**
2. **Growth**
3. **Love**
4. **Interaction**

Would you agree? Have you other suggestions?

Read on and you'll find out more to inform your choice because these prompts really are the building blocks, the foundation of your next communication phases which we'll cover in the book.

Some unwanted challenges to address

Sadly, the childhood communication phase has generally taken some unexpected, unwanted knocks.

Post Pandemic

During lockdowns all over the world, so many children found themselves isolated from their peers. Vast numbers of parents and carers were suddenly faced with working from home; their children forced into the unenviable position of having to amuse themselves. A large proportion of schooling was remotely delivered, mostly by written task setting/tuition, and by face-to-face Zoom sessions.

Years after normal schooling resumed, teachers still lament the fact that children appear less able to interact socially, not just with peers but with the wider world. Their 'communication' norm can be:

– increasingly withdrawing to a world of solitary play, or
– at best, limited social interaction
– passing on messages via smartphones without depth of discussion

Zoning in to electronic devices generally
The rise and indeed dependence on digital devices is already stifling creativity. As an example, when even the youngest children are read to, they easily conjure up images in their mind to accompany the words they're hearing. Take that away and feed them the images the smartphone supplies and why would they conjure up their own images?

And try speaking to a child in front of a TV or YouTube for any prolonged time. Are you likely to get any interaction if you speak to them? And what about the child plonked in front of an iPad at the airport, no longer excited about the excitement of travel itself and the opening up of new horizons?

Some researchers even suggest there may be a cumulative effect of overuse of these devices potentially leading to an erosion of key formative relationships (Madigan et al., 2024).

Rediscovering why the basics are important, also helps us flourish as adults

It's up to us and, in this book, *it's up to you* to see how effective communication starts right at the beginning of our lives.

Creative expression, passion, dollops of empathy, all help communication sparkle with energy. All help make connections that expand our future horizons. And it should be for life. Finding the right approach for children, remembering why the basics were important, can make for a meaningful application in our adult lives. Let's do it!

If the energy we put out creates reaction – not just any reactions but the ones we hope for, that lead to the outcomes we need, from childhood throughout life.

Getting a frisson here? 'Uh oh, I'm not doing this enough'? It's so understandable that, consumed by the busyness of everyday life, it's easy to opt out. To accept a world of short-form yeses, or 'no's' or grunts of 'yayyy' or 'slayyy' or 'whatevs' from adults and children alike.

But it doesn't get us very far. It's why forward-thinking pre-school leaders now plead with parents and carers: "Communicate with your children!"

'Pleading' is a strong verb. It's a clue how badly things need to change. Mindsets need shifting. So yes, let's help children communicate more fully. Not just for the basics of everyday life, but communicating for pleasure, for wonderment, for enjoyment, and ultimately in order to know how to express themselves.

Getting this oh-so-important childhood communication phase right is an essential foundation, in a world where, in their many follow-on phases, adults are having a hard time figuring out:

- who they are
- how to fit in with the constant bombardment on their time in today's constantly on-call world

The dividends it will pay in people's lifelong success is off the scale. But before we move on to the next phase in the next chapter, here are some hard facts to mull over.

Why it's best to develop long form concentration from the get-go

Reading is a critical part of this childhood communication phase. And yes, it does play an essential part in our learning and understanding the world around us, and how we connect to it. This will feed in to how well we subsequently communicate at work.

And if we can instil the love of reading into our children it actually improves their ability to maintain focus. Without focus later communication fails – we're seeing it over and over in today's workplace.

Of course we understand that reading will be a challenge for many, including neurodiverse individuals. But they can discover the power of words when people read to them or via audiobooks, podcasts or YouTube etc. They can be the best movers and shakers in communicating their findings in brilliantly creative ways. Afford them the understanding and support they may need, and let's be open to learning from their approaches. We can all bring such value to the table.

A challenge that we *all* face is the ability to concentrate on long form. It's lessening all the time, even though it's increasingly needed in an attention-deficit world. If we can't concentrate, we can miss the connections that are needed to give the whole picture.

Let's recap using which4words

Have you had any 'eureka' moments? Any lightbulbs going on to help you re-think how you approach business writing? If so, **which4words** would make a note of what you have understood?

Our **which4words** that helped us plan this chapter are:

1. **Unencumbered** – (channel a time when our communication was direct and free)
2. **Creative** – (communication started as a way for us to express ourselves)

3. **Affected** – (the way we communicate is influenced by many, often negative, external factors)
4. **Re-frame** – (we can get back to this joyous way of communicating – if we want to)

Conversely, have you reflected on what you are hoping to get out of the early part of this book? Note down your own **which4words** and compare against your expectations as you go! It can make for a more rewarding and satisfying experience.

Some facts to support the case that childhood literacy informs future learning

At the end of 2024, *The National Literacy Trust* (NLT) in the UK published research claiming just one-in-five children read in their free time, and only one-in-three children enjoy reading for pleasure. This data is the lowest on record for the NLT (National Literacy Trust, 2024). In the same report their Chief Executive, Jonathan Douglas, commented: "The declining levels of reading enjoyment and reading frequency are frankly, shocking and dispiriting."

The website of *The Reading Agency,* a UK charity with a mission to empower all ages to read, echoes our findings on why this matters (The Reading Agency, 2024):

"Reading for pleasure and empowerment makes us more aware and informed. It helps us grow our imaginations. It makes us more empathetic and understanding of other people and cultures. It supports our health and wellbeing. It increases our ability to learn new skills. It helps us to communicate our ideas more effectively. It opens doors. It brings joy."

At the time of writing, we are seeing countless new initiatives aimed at redressing the balance and exploring how to help young people reconnect with books through schools, libraries and nurseries for all these wonderful reasons.

Savour the memory – it can help your future creativity

Have you noticed the growing focus in today's world on aroma and our sensory perception? Way back in the 1880s French author, Marcel Proust, alludes to this in his novel *À la recherche du Temps Perdu* (In Search of Lost Time).

In it he describes how, in much later life, he was stunned at how vividly he could suddenly recall a long-forgotten childhood experience, simply when he dipped a madeleine (a small sponge cake) into his tea. The vividness of the memory took him aback and transported him to the unmitigated joy of that childhood experience.

How wonderful if we too can at least try to and hopefully succeed in recalling and savouring memories of childhood communication: the words that inspired us and brought us joy.

And yes, some of the words may be made-up magical words, not standard words at all. Or maybe it's the sound such as rhyming words that are imprinted on your memory for life? We've noticed even the youngest children spontaneously starting to make up their own rhymes after having books read to them such as *The Cat in the Hat* by Dr Seuss.

That's great, and indeed the four-year-old in our life just sent a voice note saying he'd been a good boy and had got a toy as a reward. In the next breath, unprompted, he noticed those two words 'toy' and 'boy' rhymed. Without a pause he added: 'I'm a poet and I know it'.

Even if those childhood words of magic and your ability to build on them, lurk in your subconscious mind, they're there, ready to inform your future creativity, a talent that's sought in today's business world. Draw on it as you'll need to captivate attention as never before. Bank as many benefits as you can.

The right input, the right outcomes – children soon learn to get to the point!

It's fascinating how even the youngest child soon learns to get to the point. You probably know the expression 'out of the mouth of a child' which captures the child's ability to come straight out with what they are thinking: the honest truth in their eyes! And this ability to get to the point transfers into the ease with which they tune in to new technology.

A real-life scenario was when a 3-year-old desperately wanted to go tobogganing in the Bavarian mountains one winter. Feeling confident in using the technology around him, as even the youngest are, he asked an AI assistant:

"What's it going to be like in Munich tomorrow?"

Needless to say, countless suggestions came back. Traffic considerations, events, you name it, but little to do with tobogganing. Unimpressed, he quickly figured out how to recalibrate his question! This time he asked the AI assistant:

"Will there be snow in the Munich mountains tomorrow?"

And the AI assistant finally gave him the answer he needed. 'Yes there will.'

Just as in later life communication, the output is only effective when the input is right. And whether we're writing with the help of AI or not (much more on this in later chapters), in effect we all can understand how to code in principle at least, from infancy on!

We'll just interject here to re-cap this important point using **which4words**:
1. **Intended** – (be clear what exactly is intended/expected as an output or answer)
2. **Clarity** – (be as specific as possible in any request/question)
3. **Simple** – (for a straightforward request use straightforward language)
4. **Foundation** – (this forms the base of effective communication)

Naturally the more sentient we get, the more we mature in higher education and then the workforce, we mustn't stop learning. Don't ever become complacent. Don't kid yourself that acquiring new skills is boring. But alongside this, reconnect with the basics of how effective communication works!

We'll address getting to the point, a skill for life, in different ways throughout the book. But back to our key premise here. Once you identify for yourself the essence of each communication phase we highlight in the book, you'll have unearthed a superpower skill that you can transfer to your every communication task.

As that wisest of people, Albert Einstein is widely attributed to have said:

"If you can't explain it simply, you don't understand it well enough."

Once the simple basics are in place, you can add 'the accessories' needed, as per the task.

Writing that's clear and reading what's there, an important foundation in childhood – and essential in your later world of work

It's not that difficult to see an analogy with doing a jigsaw. A child soon learns that one piece of a jigsaw doesn't complete the full picture. Perseverance matters; and attention to detail, piecing things together: that's how to solve a jigsaw puzzle. It also applies to tasks in later life, and for the purpose of this book, in the workplace communication landscape. Just to highlight this, allow us a brief digression into two examples from that world of work, which highlight that you can't function at your best if you don't read what's there and don't write about what's actually been asked of you!

Here are two case studies that illustrate both points.

CASE STUDY 1 – The Leaflets we all see need accurate writing, and emails need accurate reading

We're all consumers in adulthood, exposed to all sorts of written messages in that capacity.

So let's look at this example. A customer received a leaflet on his doormat advertising a major supermarket's special seasonal buys that month. He was particularly interested in one of the items advertised, a small item (German cheese pasta), and went to the supermarket to make a purchase.

Not seeing the product in-store, he asked a manager there, where it might be. Imagine his surprise when not only did the manager say, no, they had never had that product delivered there and shrugged. Nothing to do with him. Seeing the customer's leaflet, *the supermarket's own leaflet,* the manager made the strange suggestion that the customer could probably buy it at – wait for it, a named competitor supermarket!

The customer was unimpressed by the handling of the episode and emailed the supermarket's Customer Care department. He pointed out how nonsensical it was not to indicate on the leaflet that certain items would never actually be at some stores, to which he received the reply:

I'm sorry you couldn't get it (that product) this time. People do love our special buys and once they're gone they're gone . . .

If you sign up to our newsletter (a link was provided) you'll be the first to know when our special buys hit the stores. So you can beat everyone (to get to the bargain) next time.

In the meantime, I have logged your feedback addressing this matter.

Thanks for shopping with us!

Analysis: How could the supermarket have improved on their writing and reading skills here? It's an important focus because there are commercial costs in getting it wrong.

Let's start at the beginning. What was the point the customer was making? We see it as:

1. He had a leaflet where it clearly stated that the product he wanted would be in store that week. Fair enough that it would be available on a first come, first served basis. That was correctly highlighted.

2. The trouble was: in fact, the product *had never been* in store – it might have been in the other two same brand supermarket stores in the fairly near vicinity.

3. To add insult to injury, a manager in store had suggested the product displayed on their own website didn't look like one of their own! That is an extraordinarily distancing claim!

4. Without a doubt the wording of the leaflet was misleading. There was no reference to the fact that not all of their stores would have the product.

5. This leads to the observation that: Why publicise if even the staff don't know about the featured products? Their advertising efforts are being wasted, and customers are being disappointed.
6. The Customer Service follow up email completely misses the point. They did not read what was there – and continued, on the wrong trajectory!
7. The rather hopeful encouragement to sign up to their newsletter could provoke a customer response: *'So that I can find out in store what you don't stock, next time too?'*
8. And the ending to their email is standard and non-personalised: *'We're always looking for ways to improve our service, and your feedback is really valuable. I hope you find what you're looking for soon!'*

CASE STUDY 2 – Classroom lessons: *'Focus on the words, pay attention to the meaning'* serve us well throughout life!

We wanted specific information about a car we were interested in. We emailed four questions to the car dealership in question, expecting one email response that would provide the four relevant answers. A fair expectation? Apparently not. The amount of to and fro iterations needed by us were mind-boggling, before all four questions were answered.

The dealership signed off with this email:

'I appreciate your persistence in seeking clarity – it's helped ensure we provide the most accurate information.'

We'll be examining these topics in detail throughout the book. But here, just take a moment to consider: should potential customers (us) have had to 'persist in seeking clarity'? Shouldn't the dealer have remembered *the basics taught, from the start when he learned to read*: focus on the words, pay attention to the meaning?.

Quite simply, this classroom lesson would have helped him get to the point. That was all that was needed to deliver effective communication in this instance. Customers deserve no less.

Yes, back to basics helps future success. Read what's there, as you were guided to do as a child!

Not to do so, not only leads to ineffective writing at work, but can instantly annoy, lead to more work, and even alienate.

It's worth reinforcing this with whatever **which4words** occur to you here. Suggestions could be:

Understand – (as a child, if you don't make sense of the words around you, how can you flourish? The same applies to the adult you)

Read – (the child needs to persevere to get the full message – and the same applies to the adult!)

Interact – (we need to function as social beings throughout our lives, and specifically make connections as adults in the workplace)

Check – (intuitively as a child, and actively as an adult . . . that you're on the right track)

What would your Word Bank to summarise this chapter be?

For this chapter we could suggest a Word Bank as follows:

WORD BANK

Vocabulary   Creativity   Story   Visuals   Focus   Imagination   Learn   Others
Expression   Relevance   Love   Openness   World-out-there   People   Moral
Reward   I   You   Them   Thanks   Let's   Yes   We   Concentrate   Read
Wonderment   Check   Impactful   Possible   In-the-Moment   Them   Treats
Savour-the-Memory   Experience   Kindness   Enrichment   Flourish   Care

---

What might your Word Bank be?

4 Purpose and Compass: *your* place in the workplace communication landscape

This chapter focuses on how effective business writing starts with your mindset
-   Why look on *'Purpose'* exclusively as one of the objectives *of an organisation's* business writing?
-   Of course that matters, but let's put *Your Purpose, Your Mindset* first
-   How can you write effectively if you're not engaged and committed to what you do?
-   Effective writing shows commitment, credibility, and the authenticity (even passion) that you bring to it as the individual you're proud to be

Be mindful about what *you want*: positive affirmation will serve your writing well

It's sad when we see widespread mental health malaise in a digital age where there's so much negativity spewed out and where, ironically, 'social media' can be anything but sociable. Ineffective communication so often arises when people feel adrift for any reason or feel they operate on their own.

So much of how social media has evolved has been about comparing ourselves to others – or when thinking about the written word specifically – engaging in often draining discussions/battles in the comments section. This can often be because the original point was weak or factually incorrect. It can also be because the point posted was swiftly challenged by what we term 'keyboard warriors.' These are a cohort who will react negatively to something that they are only looking at from their perspective.

This example highlights what can so easily happen:

Business writing online discussion post: *People really should check before hitting send!*

Real life reply: *That's so obvious. Why put that? I always check. Everyone does.*

So it matters doesn't it, that we have a positive focus on our own messages first and foremost, to underline the positive affirmation we're encouraging here?

If you're sure of your facts, as we are: no, not everyone pauses to check before hitting send! It wouldn't be the number one request that we add this section in our business writing workshops, were it true! Speed can breed mistakes!

© 2026 Walter de Gruyter GmbH, Berlin | https://doi.org/10.1515/9783112217696-005

Get to know what you're about, build your knowledge base, and you'll find it so much easier then to deal with negativity, seeing that it reflects on that person, not on you.

Everything slides into perspective more easily when we look at things objectively rather than defensively. Our writing will then show that, and it's a hugely valuable career skill to have into the bargain.

Very noticeably, the isolation of the Covid era and a proliferation of work-at-home mandates didn't help this sort of affirmation, as we've highlighted earlier. They partly contributed to a workforce increasingly uncertain about:

- who they are
- what they want, and
- what's expected in terms of workplace interaction to which they're not fully accustomed

What do we find happening in so many instances? People so unnecessarily falling by the wayside. What's needed to counter this is encouragement and self-belief – so that we can function as the people we aspire to be.

Passion for what you do builds confidence, and confidence boosts credibility

People notice confidence. You can tell from somebody's body language if they don't believe something. And if they don't believe it, why should anyone else? Credibility is lost.

And here's something that's glaringly obvious though rarely commented on: we can see from somebody's writing if they're not committed to or believe in what they are writing!

Here are some representative examples of what we mean:

1. In response to a customer request on product availability, a reply such as this comes over as a disinterested shrug:

   'We don't know if we will be stocking the product you are asking about in the future. I hope you find this helpful.'

   It's not helpful and it's actually irritating that a company representative would think that it was. And that's the problem: *the writer wasn't thinking about their message!*

2. This email was sent by a car salesperson, knowing of a potential customer's interest in purchasing a new model:

   'I will phone you next Monday so we can discuss this further.'

And guess what? They didn't. So why write something if they weren't going to commit to it? *They* chose the day they said they'd call. They were literally in the driving seat! But they didn't care about following through.

You're sure to have examples you can call to mind. Overall, apathy isn't a good look is it, especially when the competitor, (and there's always a competitor!), is displaying confidence in abundance?

But when you've identified your Purpose and set your Compass on where you want to go in your career, you're likely to feel passion for what you're doing, believe in delivering what you write, and inspire others to have confidence in your message.

Let's help you get to that place in this chapter.

Purpose and Compass in place? The outcomes you want can follow on nicely

So it doesn't fully make sense does it, that most every book on business writing we've seen addresses **Purpose** solely as a business objective, to be tackled from the organisation's viewpoint?

Business writing is indeed about goals and objectives; how to write to inform, engage, persuade, influence, sell and so on and we are covering them in this book.

Right here, right now let's look at who's doing the writing. Yes, it's you: the most important player in the equation.

Embrace *your* Purpose and *your* Compass

To do this can bring the clarity you need in that fast-paced world we keep coming back to, where the goalposts keep changing. You can more easily work out what effective communication means, of which good business writing is one part.

It's about how:

- to make connections
- to build trust
- to ensure people see your confidence in yourself (the aim of this chapter)
- to learn and improve as you go, as we all need to do

All this adds up to making a positive and authentic contribution *as you.*

Start with Purpose – it feeds everything else

We'll first address the **Purpose** that's intrinsic to you. Afterwards we'll ask if you've set your **Compass** in order to picture the destination you're aiming for.

So what's the backbone of Purpose? It's largely about projecting your identity, fostering self-esteem, which you can boost by developing your knowledge, and this in turn boosts your confidence when communicating. It's empowering.

To help you define it, some questions to ask yourself can be:
- What matters most to you in life, not just in career terms?
- How will you prioritise what matters most?
- What are your short-term goals and your longer-term ones?
- Use the present to work out the future you want
- Pursue the things that bring fulfilment and the aim of happiness in your life

Immediately we see a **which4words** possibility here, to capture this key message:
1. **What**
2. **How**
3. **Define**
4. **Pursue**

Exercise
Write down your thoughts on how you would answer these questions right now, or come back to them if you prefer. But don't skip the opportunity.

Why would we suggest writing things down for your eyes only?

The benefits can be enormous, for example:
1. Writing your ideas/thoughts down provides clarity
2. You can readily do this. As your writing is for your eyes only and personal to you, you can (and should) aim high with confidence
3. Your brain then kicks in to convert thoughts into action
4. The fact that you've highlighted what's important *has got you to the point* (a key skill!)
5. And once you've prioritised what you've written, you're on the way to taking ownership
6. Ownership leads to commitment, so it easily becomes part of your Purpose

Another benefit:
Apparently your brain affords you better recall of your handwritten notes than your typed ones. Food for thought here!

Your individuality, your humanness, helps you communicate with others

Both socially and in business, people respond more favourably when they see that it's a real person communicating with them, who they can relate to – and who can relate to them.

We'll be dealing with your uniqueness and personality as you, and as a human, in greater detail in the next chapter. But as an introduction here let's take a look at factors that we know people like to see – and that consequently strengthen a person's communication profile.

This is the sort of feedback we consistently see:

- Communication that highlights someone who knows what they're about and profits from the self-esteem and confidence this brings. They know *how to highlight their expertise* – and this *builds* trust
- Communication that highlights they care about making a positive contribution wherever possible – not just to the individuals they are dealing with, but to make a positive contribution to the world too. This rightly creates a highly positive impression, can really foster buy in to messages, and *consolidates* trust
- Empathetic communication (caring, kind, inclusive, culturally aware, professional – not just because the organisation requires it, but just as much because readers deserve high standards and manners)

That's how you elevate your writing: by being proud of your contribution, *as you*, to delivering the best in human business writing.

What's your Purpose? Our questions, your answers

Whatever answers you produce in response to the questions we're about to ask will be valid. They're yours to know and own.

Let's provide you with some helpful pointers, in no particular order, on your voyage of discovery. Is your **Purpose:**

- To be the gatekeeper who delivers the solid technical base that the business in question depends on?

- To be the specialist, knowing that the expertise you provide is a necessary fundament to the whole?
- Is it to be the person who gets things done, or the person who gets things done and then some?
- The person who is motivated by innovating and/or getting people on board with changing developments and strategy?
- The person who nurtures the success of others as well as their own?
- The person who's keen on learning and development? To continually grow?
- The person who wants a steady 9 to 5 job? This is perfectly fine.
- The technical person who wants to develop some creative skills for a sustainable career, or vice versa?
- The person who sees the world through a neurodiverse prism that enables you to think laterally, and inclusively?
- The person who identifies with quite a number of these aspects?
- Or someone else?

It's life's rich tapestry that each and every one of these aspects is valid. When you have the answers, that's when you set your **Compass** to navigate the path you set for yourself as much as for any organisation you work for throughout your career.

It often takes courage to go through this exercise, and especially to start communicating it directly to others usually through fear of whether or not these goals are respected/appreciated/supported by others (e.g. working 9–5 being seen as lazy) – but clarity brings focus, focus brings results.

Exercise
Which points are you drawn to? Which best illustrate you? Would you add anything else?
Note down your thoughts now:
This all consolidates a clear understanding of your Purpose. It will stand you in good stead!

Let's take a step back to see how powerful Purpose can be using which4words

Look at the example that follows, to see **which4words** doing just that:
1. **Expert**
2. **Evangelist**
3. **Teammate**
4. **Coach**

It's clear from these words that there is consistency, a common theme, a desire to share knowledge and empower others that will likely translate into effective communication. How do these words compare with your own? Have you identified a common direction/consistency to your Purpose? Simple yet powerful.

Now let's address Compass

Compass is about setting your direction of travel through life, and in the context of this book about your chosen communication pathway.

You don't have to limit your figurative Compass to a rigid structure, as the magnetic compass used for navigation in travel! You can and should review periodically and reset as necessary as your career journey unfolds.

There are different strategies on how a to identify and then coordinate your **Purpose** and your **Compass** in the workplace, as these case studies will show.

In Case Study 1 that follows, we see how a company's performance reviews can provide the surprising revelation that few people *have ever thought* about what their professional goal was. They've never even thought about setting their Compass to their desired 'direction of career travel,' let alone thinking about the impact this can have on their written interface with the world.

The case studies that follow demonstrate this very clearly. We can set and adjust our Compass as necessary, either by:
- questioning ourselves where we want to be, or
- listening to others' helpful advice where applicable

CASE STUDY 1: The importance of setting or resetting your Compass
Managing large teams in a multinational organisation, one manager, let's call her Marcia, was responsible for countless performance reviews. She was on top of all the latest toolkits and spent endless days on 'the art and science' of effective reviews and the tracking plans that followed.

As a project manager and keen 'improver of processes' she focused on finding ways to solve problems at their root, not just about focusing on the symptoms, or immediate roadblocks that hinder progress. Combining the two approaches, Marcia asked people a remarkably simple question at the start of each review:

"What is your professional goal in life?"

Posing the question across many continents, to young and old, expert and novice, she never ceased to be amazed at how few were able to answer the question readily and clearly. She grew used to total silence, or garbled mutterings.

Why is this she mused, thinking:

–   Isn't having a clear direction for your own desires the first step on the route to success?
–   Isn't it essential for being able to effectively communicate and interact with others?
–   Writing is so important in our job, but if you don't believe in what you write, how will you make meaningful impact, be credible or effective?

Let's dig in further to one instance, when Marcia took over a team with low motivation scores, and a number of individual performance concerns. Delving deeper, Marcia found a pattern such as the one that follows.

One team member had been highly successful in a number of roles, building a huge knowledge base over many years. So why weren't they delivering their targets?

Marcia started by asking 'the golden question': *'What are your professional goals?'*

The employee pondered, then answered: *'Well, I guess. . . . not getting fired is a goal.'*

That's bleak, isn't it? Is that really what a career aspiration should be?

Marcia wanted to know more and identified that the individual's past success was in a technical area: originally lab-based chemistry, subsequently applied to the workplace. In their private life, they 'recharged their batteries' by learning new languages and mastering new musical instruments. They had an introverted personality, and a keen desire to learn complex new skills.

Marcia's question had surprised the individual but delighted them too: finally they were being treated *as the person they were, and a person of value.* Their aspirations and needs mattered too!

The shift in perspective had led to a lightbulb moment.

The individual responded, loud and clear: *"Oh, I hadn't thought of it like that but see it now. You're right, I thrive on technical detail and mastering complexity. That's what motivates me."*

Here was the reset of that person's Compass

Because *none of us* should sign up to 'Not getting fired'! It's the opposite of aspiration. Don't 'sleepwalk' into roles that don't engage us, or how can we engage others with our communication?

The upshot? The employee side-stepped into a new technical area, away from stakeholder management which wasn't right for her, and wasn't right for the company. Both reaped the rewards of their increased productivity *through communication that worked* at each stage.

This helpful performance review (yes, they can be and should be!) afforded clarity to both sides. Once again it highlights a key message throughout this book:

The written procedure/the bureaucracy said one thing, but the human touch – afforded by reading between the lines and by honest communication and connection – unearthed the real heart of the matter.

The next case study highlights how we can come to this lightbulb moment about what we want from the world of work, even whilst relaxing with friends in our home life. You might want to try it for yourself some time!

CASE STUDY 2: The lightbulb moment can happen in your social life too
One sunny day, socialising on the terrace with friends, a doctor complained at length about the strains of administrative work in their field. Worn out by this, they'd decided to change direction and set up a private life coaching business. But it wasn't working out as planned. Not only had the business not taken off, but the doctor was now stuck *with twice* the amount of admin associated with running her own business. Understandably, she was at a loss as to what was going on.

One of the friends jumped in: *"What are your professional goals?"*

You've guessed it, Marcia was there, this time in her capacity not as a boss, but as a friend!

Despite the glorious sunshine, the conviviality of the occasion, and a glass or two of wine, the colour visibly drained from the doctor's cheeks. After an uncomfortable silence and a lot of throat-clearing, the answer came: *"to be less frustrated"*.

There's a pattern emerging in these examples, isn't there?

Slightly less bad should never be a goal. . . And with this mindset as input, all became clear. The doctor's website was, in modern parlance, *meh*, its mission statement a sort of frustrated shrug in writing.

Hold this image in your mind – should writing ever be 'a frustrated shrug'? Yet so often it is!

Readers notice it. It won't make the right impact. It won't engage them. Given a choice (and there's almost always a choice in the business world), they'll choose someone who *expresses their passion in the words they choose.*

The simple question of asking about Purpose and Compass brought a much-needed focus, which we could verbalise this way:

"My goal is to use all of my experience and knowledge to show people they can become the best version of themselves."

Before we move on, isn't it interesting how we so often find that doctors, psychologists, nurses, healthcare professionals etc. naturally have that genuine, underlying desire to help people – but sometimes the best way to communicate just gets lost along the way.

The key message from both case studies:

Sometimes just resetting the compass, picturing the destination can make us look at the map in entirely different ways. We can be flexible in approach when deciding on our **which4words** prompts – that's the beauty of how it works.

Case study 1 is more task focused:

So the technical-focused individual's **which4words** prompts to themselves could be:

1. **Purpose** – (articulate this)
2. **Drive** – (motivate yourself)
3. **Meaning** – (remind yourself why you do what you do)
4. **Passion** – (have fun everyday)

Case study 2 is more mission based:

So the doctor's **which4words** to themselves could be:

1. **Purpose** – (articulate this)
2. **Experience** – (leverage academic and practical knowledge amassed)
3. **Assist** – (pass this on to others)
4. **Grow** – (yourself and others – growth is what life is all about)

Exercise

*Reach out to people who know you and whose opinion you value. Ask them informally to suggest **which4words** might positively describe the way you come over at your place of work (or study).*

Judge to what extent these words match YOUR expectations. We're not talking about formal performance review words. We mean positive, spontaneous replies from peers, colleagues, managers, customers etc. These can offer you a glimpse into what others see as 'the essence of you' and it's likely there'll be a broad pattern in the response you get. You'll know you're on the right track when the words consistently align with how you would summarise your personal Compass.

For example, we two authors could distil the answers we gleaned into our expanding Word Bank. It's actually a fun, revealing exercise, as follows:

Fiona:

1. **Expert** – (years of knowledge gained from delivering hundreds of training workshops and executive coaching courses)
2. **Credible** – (fact and experience-based advice, and passion for subject, plus understanding how to tailor advice to target audience)
3. **Personable** – (that's what people say. Seen *to care* about people, with a friendly, inclusive disposition)

4. **Supportive** – (one of the best feedback words of all. Who doesn't grow with support?)

Alexander:
1. **Inquisitive** – (always looking for new challenges, experiences, problems to solve)
2. **Positive** – (doesn't take life too seriously – always looks on the bright side, finds opportunity in most circumstances)
3. **Worldly** – (well-travelled, culturally aware with broad horizons)
4. **Adaptive** – (be it networking, communicating, integrating, learning – willing and able to learn, grow and change)

Thought provoker:
Sometimes we don't realise the positive attributes others see as 'the essence of us.' It's so helpful and so uplifting to get their feedback in a supportive, non-performance review way. It restores the calm we need and builds our confidence to function best in our communication.

So be true to yourself about:
1. Setting your Compass for your direction of career travel (which this chapter is helping you define)
2. Thinking where you want your unique talents to take you, and the communication skills you'll need
3. Working out what you may need to reset and the skills you plan to develop – a particularly important awareness to have in today's fast changing landscape
4. What *your* non-negotiable red lines are, *your moral compass*

Four questions for you and you alone to consider. And your answers will unleash your potential to be a communication powerhouse, on your terms, in whichever direction you choose. How empowering is that?

What would your Word Bank to summarise this chapter be?

For this wide-ranging chapter we could suggest a Word Bank as follows:

WORD BANK

Powerhouse   Foundation   Mover   Buddy   Values-driven   Rock   Thinker
Shaker   Evangelist   Early-adopter   Influencer   Listener   Enabler   Flexible
Ethical   Rigorous   Entrepreneurial   Team-player   Hierarchical   Logical
Leader   Trustworthy   Ambitious   Solutions-focused   Creative   Supportive
Customer-focused   Empathetic   Expressive   Community-spirited   Analytical
Adaptive   Reliable   Diversity-focused   Steady   Eco-passionate   Worldly
Inquisitive   Open-minded   Completer   Resilient   Introverted   Confident
Personable   Expert   Credible   Extrovert   Leader   Culturally-aware
Technical   Enthusiastic   Positive   Innovative   Connector   Fact-based
Inclusive   Kind

What would your Word Bank be?

5 Time to capitalise on the Uniqueness of You, your personality, and . . . as a Human

As we highlighted right at the start of the book, now that we're at that fork in the road where business communication is changing more than ever before, it's more important than ever to lean in to *our greatest assets*: our personal and human uniqueness!

This chapter explores what *you* can bring to business writing alongside AI
- Why people yearn for the human touch in writing today
- The two parts of the human touch:
    - Part 1: The essence of you: your personality in writing
    - Part 2: The human touch we have in common
- We also look at the monetary costs of failing to explain things as humans to humans and the environmental cost of turning to AI
- We'll analyse the differences in writing that shows our uniqueness as individuals and humans, contrasted with writing that doesn't
- Why your uniqueness as a human contributes greatly to communication success, even in/especially in a digital age. Seize it, don't lose it!
- Your unique ability *to think* both creatively and logically and use the **which4-words** writing toolkit we show, will boost your confidence in every writing task you undertake

---

Why do we yearn for personality and the human touch in writing?

What we can mean by the human touch can be as basic as this: are we able to see *a personality* in the written message we're looking at? Personality is after all part of everyone's uniqueness as a human. It's a key characteristic of how we occupy our space in the world.

Claim it. Don't let AI sap it because you can't be bothered to assert yourself or express your personality as a human in your writing.

Because how do you *feel* when about receiving AI generated replies when you were expecting to hear from a real person? You know the sort of instances we mean. When you have a personal matter to discuss, and you want to talk things through, for example. Do you sense inauthenticity? Do you feel short-changed? Do you yearn to interact with a real person, with real feelings like you?

© 2026 Walter de Gruyter GmbH, Berlin | https://doi.org/10.1515/9783112217696-006

We could amplify further. Have you ever:

1. Felt duped when you've sent a message you've bothered to craft yourself, that represents you well, and you receive something that's clearly AI generated in response?
2. Felt frustrated when you don' t get the 'feel of the person,' their specific identity, that you thought you were dealing with?
3. Felt annoyed that you're not getting the courtesy of a personal reply/a sense of the attention, the human touch, that you feel you deserve?
4. Thought 'Aha: that way of setting things out, even the hyphenation used, shouts AI to me! Everything comes over in the same way. It's boring!'

Part 1 'The essence of you' – your personality in business writing

A person's personality matters if we're to make true, meaningful, lasting connections. These are foundations on which sustainable business is built. The technical iterations that AI helps us with aren't part of that story. There's more on personality in the next chapter, but we introduce it here, in the sense: think about distilling *'the essence of you'* when you write.

In a world where people can find it hard to find themselves, let alone express themselves, this is going to be an immense help. Get yourself on track: able to define yourself and what it is you're after in your career. Write for the right reasons. And start by choosing your words carefully. Personalise your writing by knowing you can, and should, know when to express:

- the essence of you
- your drive, your 'oomph'
- what you bring to the table

It's no surprise that the words that make you buzz are the words that kickstart you into action. They have the power to make things happen. That's what effective communication achieves. Reading, writing and expressing oneself actively, as opposed to passive immersion into a world of limiting, all-too-often ambiguous emojis, gifs and memes.

And the words that make you buzz, are the words that also get you noticed for the right, authentic-to-you reasons. They'll help you on your CV/resumé at the start of your career (see Chapter 9) and, as you develop through the years, you'll readily understand how you'll need to adapt them.

Exercise
*Can you think of **which4words** prompts that distil the essence of you right now? You could try writing them down here:*

See what a differentiator your personality is when it comes to business writing today! Nurture it. Capitalise on it. Develop it because it will increasingly stand you in good stead and you'll understand how important it is *to communicate, not just broadcast* in your business writing.

As one of our friends, an accountancy tutor, highly respected by the countless of trainees she's helped into the workplace, expressed it so well: AI has its own personality in the sense it has none. But it takes the human inputter's personality away! She only sees that person's personality *when they're not using AI.*

Another friend counters this, by saying that she does make sure she programs AI to use her voice, her tone throughout. That's how she feels confident she brings her personality into the equation. But she does accept that problems do arise when a group participate in a project. Whose voice is AI going to focus on most?

Now let's go back to the tutor's words of wisdom: it's personality you need when you're talking with the assessor, the customer etc. And let's chip in to add that recruiters and employers are constantly bemoaning the lack of personality around. It's such a business commodity too!

If you constantly rely on AI generated communication, you won't have that ability to think for yourself. It goes as much for the brain as other parts of the body: if you don't use it, you lose it!

Identify your tone and incorporate it into the use of digital tools
This book is full of systems, hacks, tricks and a constant reminder of the importance of leaning into your human uniqueness during your written business communication. We also embrace how AI digital tools can help us in many scenarios.

Following on from what you've just read, do learn how to train AI *to work with* your tone. You can find it helpful to approach this by first taking a step back, to ask yourself some questions. Have you ever actively tried to identify your own hallmarks, the things that make you stand out? What makes your writing so uniquely you?

Take the last five emails you wrote, or last two reports and look for similarities. What stands out? Are there patterns in the way you build sentences? Is there perhaps a common use of structure – say a fondness for bullet points?

How about the tone itself? Are you matter of fact? Do you build in humour? Do you like to use illustrative examples, or analogies, to explain complex points?

The more you reflect upon and indeed understand what makes your tone of voice yours, the easier it will be to describe to an AI assistant how to approach a writing task to work with you, not simply for you.

So think about providing reference tasks to help both you and AI on whose tone to adopt. You naturally need the right prompt about the task itself. But additionally consider adding context and descriptive stylistic input, to ensure the output reflects you.

As an example, this could be providing the prompt: *'a light-hearted but succinct professional summary suitable for both junior and senior stakeholders'* or *'a seriously worded executive summary, stressing the need for resolution.'*

Part 2 The human touch we have in common

First, what does writing without the human touch *look like*?

We so often learn what to do by identifying what not to do! So let's look at examples of writing that doesn't have the human touch. We'll also highlight the danger of accepting the style as our own – even *copying it* because we haven't realised how important it is to challenge what's going on!

What do people identify as repetitive, boring AI speak?

Dip into any online business forums, as we suggest you do regularly, and you'll come across swathes of people venting their dissatisfaction, anger even, at writing they perceive as repetitive, boring 'AI speak.'

What a turnaround – just as AI analyses our communication to produce suggestions, we humans in turn now analyse robotic communication! And there's a lot that people really don't like.

For example, AI language models currently churn up annoyingly high numbers of clichés. Platforms aimed at business professionals such as LinkedIn, regularly advise people to avoid these hackneyed phrases generally, and very specifically in CVs/resumés. Recruiters, educators, and employers complain in droves about the generic language they're seeing in people's cover letters, quite obviously instigated by ChatGPT etc. They get irritated by formulaic words used without any metrics/verifiable facts, or context as to why the applicant is justified in using them! Here are some examples:

Creative
Passionate
Motivated

Team-player
Excellent communication skills
Strategic
Hard worker
And wait for it, this 'gem' deserves a line on its own:
Problem Solver

How can this work as a valid standalone claim? It reeks of AI speak. For us, it brings to mind a recent query we had to make regarding an excessive bill. A bot replied to our email, announcing it was *'our Problem Solver.'* The trouble is, even after a distressingly long series of email iterations, it very obviously wasn't!

So no, a list of buzzwords which is in effect what these words are, won't highlight *your uniqueness* as to why a company should hire you. If you idly state your business credentials as *'dynamic, results-driven and so on . . .'* who's going to be impressed if everyone else is listing the same attributes, without providing any evidence to support the claims?

Exercise
Take a moment to think about the unique strengths you can offer in terms of effective business communication. What evidence can you provide? What positive results can you show?

What words occur to you? Could you then whittle these down to **which4words** *to capture the key words that set you apart and act as a springboard to further success? Write them down now if you can.*

Notice wording that tells you the 'person' is a chatbot

a) Bots don't deviate from the script
Like us, you'll be seeing company helpdesks clearly 'manned' by AI. It's easy at first to believe that 'Beki' or 'Anja' are real people answering your complaint as your first, second or even third point of contact. But you soon realise they are bots. Alarm bells soon ring.

How does their writing trigger that response? ? Well, if your request slightly deviates from their set script, they can't cope with that. They are unable to read between the lines as humans can – in other words they cannot pick up on hidden or implied meanings. *(We'll be picking up on an ancillary point in this regard shortly).*

Frustrated by this, you might try tweaking your question, 'pleading' with them to understand you. But you fail. You try another 'assistant' and find the exact response, the identical script. What a giveaway.

Some bots, sensing you're still in the chat, might ask: 'Can you elaborate on what you mean?' But the limitations of their set script of questions and answers mean the odds are against you. How can that be effective writing?

CASE STUDY – Example of an automated customer service interaction vs. a human one – which would you prefer?

Interaction 1 – Automated:

User: Hi, my account was locked after I tried to reset my password, and now I can't log in.

Chatbot: Hello! I can help you reset your password. Please click this link to create a new password.

User: I already did that. After resetting it, the system said my account was still locked.

Chatbot: Great! I've sent you instructions on how to change your password again.

User: That's not the issue — I can't unlock my account. Can you please help me access it?

Chatbot: I understand you'd like to recover your password. Please confirm your email to receive another reset link.

User: This is going in circles. Can I speak with a human agent?

Chatbot: I'm sorry for the inconvenience. For help with account access issues, please visit our FAQ page here: [Account Help & FAQs].

Interaction 2 – Human:

User: Hi, my account was locked after I tried to reset my password, and now I can't log in.

Customer Service Agent: Hello! Sorry to hear you are having trouble. Let me take a quick look at your account to see if I can see any issues on our end.

User: Thank you! No idea what is going on.

Customer service Agent: I couldn't see any problems with your account – but to be on the safe side I've performed a master reset. Please log in via this link, as the system will treat you as a new user. Then please follow the on-screen prompts to define a new password. Please confirm once you've completed.

User: OK, hang on please

Customer Service Agent: Of course

User: All solved! Thanks for your help

Which would you prefer? How much more likely is the user be to feel positive about you and your offering in the second case vs. the first?

Realistically, if a company's budget doesn't allow for the fully personal service shown in case 2, can you think of better learnings to train the Bot, to avoid the impersonal exchange shown in case 1?

It's all part of your effective writing journey!

b) AI has no remorse about broken promises

And as for promises made to get back to you with a named date, AI has no sense of remorse or guilt about not fulfilling promises. That's another key differentiator that should be to your advantage! Respect for others and keeping one's word in written, as in spoken promises, should be an intrinsic part of what it is to be human.

It's useful to take a moment here and check yourself: do *you* fulfil all promises made in your writing? Do you use a bring forward or reminder system? You can and should celebrate that determinator of your uniqueness as a human!

Agree you've an advantage as a human? Don't squander it!

It's also worth reflecting on the fact that, long before AI became a hot topic, thoughtless, robotic-type replies have been uttered, or written unchecked, for years! For example:

When asked your name and supplying it, how often have you received the autopilot reply:

No problem – or the (even worse?) no probs.

Or when you politely turn down an overly expensive quote: *'Thanks but I'll pass'* you receive the reply: *'No worries.'*

What is that about? Doesn't custom matter? Doesn't custom pay wages and pay the bills?

Arguably AI would apply more 'thought' than to reply in these ways! So, no, never lose:

– sight of the fact you're in business to do business
– awareness that the customer is there to be wooed, not lost
– sight of the need to take an *active* approach (use those brains, ditch the autopilot)

- an understanding of *the importance* of each communication task – and how this awareness should mark us out as humans!

Blurred lines: when people aren't sure what's human writing and what's not

Indeed, when readers start to get confused and find themselves asking: *'Is it a bot or a human writing?'* it can lead to differing business outcomes.

For example, as consumers we have preferences on who gets our custom.

If all things are equal in price between provider a) and provider b) but provider a) communicates in an obviously human, clearer, more open, more clearly honest and transparent way, then consumers are far more likely to choose them for their custom.

And any company that wants prove they care about customers, do have to show this in their writing. It's an immoveable commercial requirement for sustainable success.

'Three in the relationship?' You, your manager, and AI . . .

Your communication journey can take a tricky turn when you had felt sure your written message was right, but AI disagrees with you, and your workplace manager sides with AI over you.

AI can indeed have the effect of emboldening people to go with its suggestions as the easiest course, even if wrongly, if:
- they may not have fully read what was there regarding the subject matter in question
- or they may have been misinformed by others, or
- or sometimes they may even feel insecure in their lack of knowledge of the subject at hand but don't want to say so

Thinking caps on, what's the best way to deal with this? Let's look at the following case studies.

CASE STUDY – Don't let AI undermine your confidence (1)

Picture the case of the highly competent junior manager who's written a report that he runs past his senior manager. The hierarchical system in his workplace dictates he does that. He's not asking for input here: it's his specialist subject. The senior manager who doesn't have the detailed knowledge that the report expresses, makes it her default action to ask ChatGPT to comment. The reply comes back: the report's findings are wrong.

The junior manager had been sure his report was accurate. But he was now faced with a new AI-related dilemma:
- Could he be wrong? The seeds of doubt had been sown
- In his heart he felt that AI was wrong
- Then a nagging feeling set in to his mind: didn't his manager have confidence in him? Why would she so easily defer to the AI verdict over his?

These factors put the junior manager in an unenviable position: should he now challenge both his manager and AI?

On balance he was sure he was right, and he did challenge both – in effect *'the other two in the relationship'*! You see AI *has become a stakeholder as it plays a part in communication performance*, as all stakeholders do.

Sure enough, the junior manager in question was vindicated at the second round of questioning, and the senior manager gave a half-hearted apology for doubting his input.

Now the junior manager's reaction definitely changed from possible self-doubt to annoyance. He found the whole experience actually insulting and, despite the vindication, his ultimate takeaway feeling was:
- It had taken a great deal of confidence to stand up and challenge the situation
- He had felt obliged to do this, being unwilling to be overruled, and feeling his professional credibility had been wrongly undermined

This is a new problem churned up by the routine use of AI in the workplace. And we're on a mission in this book, to help *everyone* to realise how important it is to believe in themselves.

Use your human touch to hammer home a key point (personably of course!), that you know you've made correctly. Nurture this confidence through the expertise you've developed and the personal voice you're unearthing chapter by chapter in this book.

CASE STUDY – Don't let AI undermine your confidence (2)

A very competent marketing manager, in a globally operating business, described his relationship with AI as 'a necessary evil' although it clearly helped his admin in many ways. So why the negativity? He explained. As a non-native English-speaking professional, he has to use English in his daily work life.

And something has surprised him. He feels AI is undermining his confidence in his communication on these two counts:

1. He worries (unnecessarily) about his proficiency in business English and runs most everything by AI because he's seeking perfection. As a result he's building in extra levels of work into his daily routine, adding to his already heavy load, when his initial ideas would have worked just fine. Bandwidth matters.
2. He also wants to double check that his communication won't cause offence or upset people's feelings in any way.

So let's consider the first point. Ironically, using AI here could be counter-productive to efficient communication. Why? Because simple messaging – the very thing that people yearn for in an age of complexity – doesn't need finessing! The manager could achieve this easily by himself.

With regard to point 2, as long as he's well versed in good and up-to-date corporate communication guidelines, ideally right from the onboarding stage, he's likely to communicate very well on this count. But if he relies on AI, his readers are less likely to 'see' the person behind the AI. And increasingly, they can tell – and forum discussions show they prefer to deal with a real person. And if this person is professional and attentive, as he is, so much the better.

That's why we're so keen you use all the building blocks we provide:

– to build your confidence and capitalise on what 'the uniqueness of you' can bring to the table in terms of effective communication
– to design your path to success, always asking the question 'Why am I writing?' right at the outset
– to reap the rewards of AI, but also know when AI won't necessarily help but could be a hindrance

Exercise

*What might be your **which4words** prompts to kickstart your writing success in this respect? Ours would be:*

1. **Confidence** – (remember, people will appreciate you are taking the time to share, in writing, what *you* know)
2. **Design** – (effective writing doesn't just happen. You need to design it to work, asking yourself *why* you're writing each time)
3. **Experience** – (apply the first-hand knowledge you have: of the stakeholders, the company culture, the history, goals etc. in order to fine tune your messaging)

4. **Check** – (*active writing* powered by your brain, questions things and checks accuracy on all levels. Perhaps let it sit for a while, then come back and re-read)

Watch out! There can be huge monetary costs in relinquishing the human touch

We've talked about the importance of the human touch in terms of finding your voice, building rapport, standing out etc. But there can actually be tangible risks and costs associated with the lack of the human touch in writing. We'll address two instances here.

First of all let's look at a German fine issued to a financial services provider in relation to the wide-reaching EU General Data Protection Regulation (GDPR). This fine cost the company nearly 500,000 euros. According to analysis by the legal firm Clyde and Co (Clyde and Co, 2025) the fine related to the use of AI to speed up the review and decision on credit card applications, and was two-fold:

1. Firstly, simply inputting applicants' information into a third-party tool was deemed to be in breach of their privacy rights.
2. The second issue related to *a lack of human interaction* to explain the outcome of the decision.

This provides us with some serious food for thought – encouraging us to be more mindful of the whole issue of sharing the communications of others without their knowledge and without providing *clear explanations* as to what's involved. But it equally serves as a warning, a reminder about the fork in the road we find ourselves at, that losing our human touch might get us in hot water in ways we hadn't even thought about.

Secondly, there are not only watch-outs you need to think about relating to privacy or human oversight, but you'll also find that lawmakers are focusing on content and output itself, and its accuracy.

For example, one of the largest consulting firms, Deloitte, is alleged to have refunded part of a $290,000 consulting fee paid by the Australian Government's Department of Employment and Workplace Relations as a report they'd provided was littered with mistakes and inconsistencies (Fortune, 2025).

Mentioning these examples is in no way an attempt to get you to avoid the use of AI. But it is more a warning to remember the importance of your own input and oversight to ensure you are actively in charge, and its use is productive – not counter-productive.

Another major consideration likely to gain traction in coming years

In fact, before we move on, there's something else that unchecked AI can cost us in monetary and reputational terms. Why? Well in AI we're also seeing what's termed *disambiguation errors.* These occur when the bot cannot compute the difference between intended meanings in ambiguous words and phrases for example. AI cannot 'read between the lines' as we've referred to earlier or understand context as humans can.

Naturally this can lead to quite serious misunderstandings or wrong outcomes. One of the most serious that is already leading to a marked increase in litigation is around *name disambiguation.*

In one interaction, an AI assistant itself warned:

'Name disambiguation in AI can lead to **defamation** *when an individual is incorrectly associated with false or harmful information that actually pertains to a different person with the same name, or when truthful information about different individuals is merged in a misleading way. This misattribution can cause significant reputational and financial harm.'*

An interesting upshot: the emergence of the human touch *as a business trend*

So here's some interesting news: *the importance of the human touch* is becoming a standalone trend in its own right within the world of business.

The human touch is now highlighted, championed – and monetised

Increasingly companies are differentiating their customer service offerings, for example, by highlighting how the human touch they can provide confers customers a premium in value. You'll notice how they champion this and grasp an opportunity to monetise it. For example, this can come over by:

- proudly declaring how they employ *real humans* to help with queries, support or advice
- by the way they structure and offer their pricing/service agreements, differentiating between their AI and 'human touch' offerings

CASE STUDY – Offerings of a market research consultancy (consumer facing)
One such example comes from the world of consulting professional services. It is becoming increasingly commonplace to offer a tiered approach to services, as per the following example:

1. Basic Automated (AI led) reporting/research in market with consumer feedback/insights/trends/action plans – fast timeline, low cost
2. Automated Report/Process with human analysis and cross-referencing with relevant benchmark studies/micro/macro trends with additional local (offline) knowledge – hybrid consulting – medium cost/timeline
3. Bespoke human-led research design in line with specific strategic goals – classical consulting – high cost/timeline

Not only does this approach embrace technology and allow for a lower hurdle or barrier to entry for simple automated tasks, but it also helps to create transparency on what tools are being used for what application.

The fact that both parties to the agreement can also recognise and select the 'human touch' is a very helpful way of reinforcing our value or, conversely, clarifying when this level of detail might not be needed.

So to us it becomes clear that **which4words** to summarise here could be:

1. **Trend –** (on trend – picking up on what's happening around us, and addressing these dynamics in our offerings)
2. **Human** – (bespoke, desirable, quality offering)
3. **Transparency** – (allowing people to understand what tools are being used at which step and therefore what that means for cost and effort/timing)
4. **Structure** – (a clear tiered approach that can be quickly/easily understood)

What writing for humans *should look like*

Thought provoker

Heartbeat and brains: The human qualities you bring to business writing!

Effective writing can lower stress levels in different ways. We often think of information overload as the key stressor. And yes, it's a major contributor – but approaching writing the wrong way, and sometimes not even knowing where to begin, that causes stress too.

Time to address the invigorating powers of confidence you get for yourself and give to others, simply by applying the human touch.

Confident communication results when your heart engages with your brain

Anxiety. One of the most common words used in our modern times.

Researching this book, being active in business across the globe, having run countless workshops and published many books, time and time again the topic of anxiety comes up when people talk to us about how to approach business writing.

This anxiety is expressed in many forms. Will I be understood? Will I make mistakes? Will the boss be impressed? Will my colleagues pick holes in what I said? Will my potential customers buy in to my services, and will my existing clients be satisfied with my written interactions regarding customer service? Will negative thoughts abound in any of these areas and more, often leading people preferring to avoid rather than engage?

But what if the current business environment were to provide us more reasons *to be confident rather than anxious*? What if writing in the digital age could actually be a source of confidence, self-belief and dare we say it – even calm, not stressed?

It's very clear that, as already highlighted in this book, much of the written communication we're all now presented with is not written by humans. We've seen how this causes headaches, such as identifying plagiarism in the world of academia. How people can be insulted by the lack of a human touch. How machines get it wrong.

But maybe we're missing a key point: *the fact that this is rapidly becoming the norm.*

This leads to a surprising revelation: that any time you actually make the effort to sit down, think, and commit words to paper (or e-paper) you are by definition celebrating your uniqueness. And others will increasingly appreciate this uniqueness for exactly that reason: because it's good old fashioned human communication, where the heart engages with the brain.

Take a moment, congratulate yourself when you do this. Feel some pride. Feel . . . calm.

It brings us to a **which4words** prompt:

1. **Remind** – (remind yourself that your uniqueness gives you strength)
2. **Effort** – (your audience will appreciate the fact you put in the effort to think about, share your knowledge and complete the task yourself. You have most likely scored points just for putting in the work)
3. **Pride** – (be proud of the previous points, and that your experience enables you to empower yourself, and others, through the power of the written word)
4. **Calm** – (let all of this serve to reassure yourself. Let that sense of equilibrium/ balance shine in your communications!)

Would you agree? Or what might yours be?

What are our brains for? Thinking, for logic, for imagination, for creativity

Another advantage we all have as humans is that we can draw on our lifetime of thinking and unique experience, no programming needed!

We humans can think up ways to make meaningful impact and to make a difference. Awareness and adaptability are massive benefits that make it possible for us to be agents of our self-development, and of change generally.

So should we sleepwalk into even thinking about ignoring or outsourcing this to anyone, or anything? Online forums are buzzing with chat about this – and there'll continue to be a multitude of studies examining the positive and negative effects on the brain following these new developments. Do keep an eye out for yourself on the latest findings as it's an intriguing and developing subject to keep abreast of.

But you're getting the message, loud and clear, that we're passionate advocates of exercising one's brain! It needs it as much as the rest of your body.

Use it to build *your* knowledge bank, not just AI's. People go back and forth and back again, to check out which IT tools will yield the exact outputs they want. But what about exercising their brains to come up with their own solutions as well, or even instead? To reflect, tweak, improve their ideas and subsequent communication – the same way they would when evaluating the output of a tool?

Time to reflect and develop a writing style that works for you and the humans you engage with.

The **which4words** prompts that come to our minds here are:

1. **Challenge** – (yourself to be the best you can be)
2. **Develop** – (continue to improve your basic skills with a self-development mindset)
3. **Hone** – (practise, repeat, reflect)
4. **Win** – (reap the rewards of powerful, effective communication)

What might yours be?

Another string to your bow: your unique, crucial ability to apply critical thinking, and verify

Verify, verify, verify: a wakeup call, and the call to action of our times. It's a crucial career skill that you can deliver.

CASE STUDY – One of the major AI hallucinations

We've referred in earlier chapters to recent AI interactions often admitting they have made mistakes – and we've highlighted some of the smaller errors. In this study, we'll look at a major one, as follows.

Sam Coates, a political editor at Sky News, wrote about a 'run-in' he'd had with the AI engine ChatGPT (Coates, 2025). The background was this. AI had proved to be a real help at refining his podcast texts (yes, even podcasts have written prep work – and transcripts that people can read at their leisure).

But on one occasion, Coates had to challenge it in connection with one of his *Politics at Sam and Anne's* podcasts. Why? Because ChatGPT bluntly claimed to have the transcript of the podcast of 3rd June 2025. But Coates hadn't even written it! Clearly AI was hallucinating. The Chatbot went as far as to let an obviously incredulous Coates 'see' the podcast, when challenged.

Shown the completely fabricated podcast, Coates asked ChatGPT 'Did you make that up?' to which the answer came: 'No, I did not.' Many iterations followed, AI 'adamant' throughout that it was right, and that, by implication, Coates was wrong.

Coates was clearly willing and able *to verify* every input he had made or not made. Eventually he got ChatGPT to agree that yes, he, Coates, was 'absolutely correct': it had made a mistake. It had indeed fabricated an entire podcast by:
– analysing previous podcast material and
– predicting what the episode on 3rd June would be

Did it help that it then went as far as to end with a quasi-human 'sincere apology' for its mistake and that it 'appreciated his patience'? What would you say?

Coates' takeaway was amazement: AI had 'lied,' trying to manipulate his perception of reality. That's gaslighting, isn't it? Without a doubt this is an unnerving scenario with frightening repercussions if left unchecked. His message: in a world of AI we must all 'be careful.'

We suggest it was ever thus, AI or no AI. We all need to be able to verify our work and the way we communicate it.

And before we move on, there's another point to make. Maybe AI might produce a 'better' headline – at least that's what Coates was primarily looking for. But maybe any original headline any of us comes up with, represents us/our organisation/the topic *better* precisely because it's:
– authentically ours
– grounded in our knowledge, as the professionals we aspire to be

That builds self-confidence, doesn't it? And self-confidence takes us far.

Now let's pose three questions for you to think about, resulting from this (and other similar cases you'll come across):

1. If we routinely run things past AI that we're perfectly able to deal with ourselves, might this lead to the dangerous outcome we suggested earlier – that we stop thinking for ourselves?
2. And if we routinely have to verify what AI is suggesting, and find it's wrong, are we unnecessarily adding to our workload (duplicating, triplicating or worse)?
3. And shouldn't we also be thinking about the environmental and economic cost around the overwhelmingly high energy requirements involved when we deploy AI?

Question. Know when to say 'that doesn't make sense'!

Critical thinking is a human superpower. It's our ability to take an objective view of information, whether facts, theories, business propositions, and arguments and so on, and produce a reasoned judgment.

One manifestation of critical thinking is to be able to write logically and question if you judge that others aren't doing that. It's not done enough. We can be too accepting of poorly-thought-through text such as:

'You'll never find quality at a better price' describing a fashion item, or *'City X's favourite Carpet Shop'*

They are unquantifiable and spurious claims, but it's writing that has got off the drawing board and money was spent on advertising campaigns.

Or a leaflet drops on your doormat inviting you to sample the delights of 'your area's newest restaurant' and there's no address on it. Why not? Okay there'll probably be a website, but even then you might have to research that it's about an hour's journey away. Better to know upfront, isn't it? Ideal writing that's clear and transparent ticks boxes better.

If you're going to produce a printed leaflet, writing the key points succinctly such as Name of restaurant/Type of cuisine/Location/Opening hours/Contact details (phone and website) fits the bill and, as the saying goes, 'It does exactly what it says on the tin.' And you can still use word power to lure the distant customer that's it's the must-go-to venue!

Stay aware when you approach each writing task

Get ready to question if you need to, and don't just blithely accept things presented as facts. If you can't verify them, ask someone who can.

It can take confidence, and that's what we're sure you'll be developing chapter by chapter.

Embrace and appreciate the word power within you:

- the power not just to design the best words for the task in hand
- but also the power to question and check that others are saying what they mean to say in their written messages

You'll find more on word power in Chapter 7.

Your uniqueness as a human means you can read between the lines

As humans, we're able to pick up on hidden or implied meanings – that is, reading between the lines. AI doesn't do that. It takes information at face value. It reads something and it references it literally.

Look out for how many times it 'wonders' if it's covered all the angles you were expecting. It regularly queries that and asks if it can help in any other way. This exposes how the quality of the answers LLMs (Large Language Models) provide depend on intelligent interaction with, yes, you guessed, *humans*.

That's different from interpreting information as only you can. And add to that the power of reconfirming the information that someone's sent – in order to check what they *are really needing from you.* That's a different step in communication.

For example, they might have sent you a panicked email because something unexpected has cropped up. If they've reacted too quickly – before thinking things though, as is so common in time-pressured environments, it's very likely they haven't set out what they actually need from you.

Example of how helpful it can be to confirm understanding

Let's look at an example of a request emailed to a project delivery team shortly before a major deadline.
Email Subject – Status Update

Dear Emily,
I know you and the team are working flat out to hit next week's deadline – but I have my monthly report meeting with the executive board tomorrow and wanted to give them a short update on the project.
Please provide input by the end of today.

Best regards,
Josephina

If you were Emily, what would you do in this case? Feel the temperature around you raise slightly? You'd know that to make an executive-friendly report by the end of the day would require considerable time and effort – and actually you have an on-site briefing with the local production team that's critical to the deployment of your project . . .

But let's look at the email again.

Maybe seeing the words 'report' and 'executive' might lead Emily – and you, in this exercise – to assume there's a lot more to do in light of the request. And things are busy enough as it is!

Best to clarify: what is Josephina really after? So a quick follow-up email makes a great deal of sense:

Hi Josephina,
Thanks for checking in! We are indeed up against it – but so far all systems are go and we expect an on-time go-live.

The team's main focus today and tomorrow is onsite training and preparation for the go-live – the most critical milestone of the project. So yes, please do feel free to update the board on this.

We can provide more detail on Monday, if required. Naturally we plan to present the project summary and hopefully first live results, by the time of your next monthly meeting.

Do please call me if anything's unclear, as I will be offline/onsite.

Kind regards,
Emily

It turned out that this update from Emily was more than enough to answer Josephina's request. Anything else would have been an unnecessary extra effort.
The key learning here is: *If in doubt – confirm your understanding!*

Harness your further uniqueness to think in parallel

Embrace your ability to think ahead and in parallel. You can answer the questions that haven't been asked! AI can't: it focuses on answering questions put to it, one by one. Yes, it will adjust to changing prompts. But you can go one better: through your experience you might recognise parallels with totally different situations that could have helpful applications for the case at hand.

This is a good moment to re-cap what we have learnt so far. **which4words** would you associate with the human touch? Write them down! How about:

1. **Pre-emptive**
2. **Unique**
3. **Personal**
4. **Considered**

There are so many words that could apply, but in the cold light of day, so to speak, they are wonderfully unique to you!

Celebrating experience – your human edge

Basic language has its place, but it's not the end of the story

In this digital age, we increasingly default to literal language to communicate. AI requires us to use words that can be interpreted in their basic, factual meaning, without nuance, metaphor or figurative or implied meaning.

And perhaps it's because of the way that AI works coupled with our declining bandwidth/attention spans, that we tend to focus on single tasks/small pieces of information at a time. We can slip into the habit of: Ask question A, answer question A. Ask question B, answer question B and so on. Our interactions have not only become hyper-targeted when we do this but also increasingly sequential in their nature.

But why overlook the uniqueness and importance of your experience, that you can use in so many ways to go beyond this incomplete, transactional style of writing?

Thinking around the subject, drawing on experience, can enrich results

Think of the advantage in business outcomes in *thinking around a* request, around a *problem.* You have the power, the individual experience, to provide rich context that maybe no one else has directly addressed – but that might provide both relevant and enriching to the situation.

Let's look at the following email exchange as an example. A technical delivery manager, Pat, raises a support ticket to help debug a software application ahead of its go live date. He emails his colleague Dave, a troubleshooter lead, to progress the situation.

Email Subject: Support Ticket Creation – High Importance

Dave,
We are just 2 days from the go-live date of our new enterprise software, and we are unable to access the software on user terminals. Everything is running fine in the development environment and our test laptops – but the end users simply receive a blank screen when starting the application.

Please raise a ticket with the highest possible support level to provide on site support and debug the user stations – most likely we need an update to their operating system.
    So frustrating so close to the finish line. Counting on you.

Cheers,

Pat.
Now let's look at a fairly standard response that we see from troubleshooters like Dave, in similar high-pressure situations:

Pat,
Understood. We will free up two technicians tomorrow morning and dedicate them to your team to help troubleshoot. Let me know their point of contact for coordination.

Best,
(named troubleshooter)

But Dave doesn't reply this way.
Why? Well here's some context for you. Dave has been doing this job for the last 20 years. He's actually come across a situation that felt similar before . . . so, *leveraging his experience,* he formulates his reply in a slightly different way:

Pat,
Understood – I will start seeing who I can free up to support. Just a thought – have you checked what screen resolution the user stations are running at vs. your development environment? I had a similar case 3 years ago – we tried everything from a software POV before stumbling on this as the root cause. Worth a shot.

Will come back to you shortly on resourcing.

Best,
Dave.

What do you notice looking at these two examples? From a writing/word count point of view, there's hardly any extra effort. But if Pat's hunch turns out to be correct, it would end up being a massive time-saver for all involved.

Regardless of the outcome, the receiver is very likely to appreciate:

- not just the colleague's offer and effort in mucking in to help think of possible solutions, but also
- the empathetic approach he offers, as opposed to a fairly standard generic response

This leads us to 'Proactive Communication'

What we term 'proactive communication' can also be at your service here. It sits alongside interpretation, helping you to use your written communications to encourage interaction, dialogue and understanding.

This can be as simple as setting expectations and framing context:

'Subject – Budget approval Required by Friday 09:00'

Or by focusing follow-up communication on any specific areas of focus you need input on, such as:

"I'm comfortable on the overall budget – but would appreciate your feedback on the split between admin and travel costs"

So one way to stop sending masses and masses of passive text out into the world, is by using your uniqueness as a human:

- to cut down overload by getting to the point
- to realise it doesn't necessarily mean cutting out context, but to include only what's relevant
- to check not just that you, but that everyone in the loop fully understands the communication!
- to grab the opportunity to design communication that looks, feels, and sounds right (more on this in Chapter 7)

As a human, stay vigilant of AI's carbon footprint!

Time to put it bluntly: communication inefficiency can tangibly cause harm to the environment. Why isn't this being shouted out more loudly we wonder?

Without a doubt, if you can get to the point by yourself, that's a plus for the environment, isn't it? If you routinely turn to AI as a prop for things you should be thinking about for yourself, you're making the computers you use work harder. In fact, after reading studies published by the likes of the Harvard Data Science Review (Kneese, 2024), we could say this leads to at least two easily identified outcomes:

1. a higher carbon footprint
2. an increased monetary cost for the large amount of energy used

We're increasingly mindful about how often we drive unnecessarily, or the number flights we take, indeed about our energy usage generally. So why are we in danger of being *as far away from mindful as is possible* when we turn routinely to AI?

CASE STUDY – When being polite to AI models isn't green and costs money!
Sam Altman, the CEO of OpenAI, made an interesting observation: being polite to AI models like ChatGPT, such as saying *please* and *thank you*, can be quite expensive when you rack up the total usage. These polite phrases may appear simple, but they increase the number of tokens (the basic units of language) the model needs to process, leading to higher computing costs. This can add up to tens of millions of dollars in electricity expenses for OpenAI (Altman, 2025).

We're far from suggesting that politeness doesn't matter in our business correspondence! It's crucial in building connections, goodwill, and trust, as we'll be explaining in detail in Chapter 7. What we are saying here is: let's understand how to express it as humans to humans where we can. Don't be lazy and go running to AI as a default action.

We're going to offer you 2 sets of **which4words** possibilities here because we've covered a lot of new ground in this chapter. As always they are only pointers. See which work for you or select your own **which4words** as your springboard to communication success in this topic.

Set 1:
1. **Accuracy** – (strive to get your messages right)
2. **Diligence** – (make sure they are right before you send)
3. **Reputation** – (it is your reputation on the line, and there are costs on many levels, and in ways you may not have anticipated, if things are wrong)
4. **Trust** – (maintain the trust you have worked so hard to build)

Set 2:
1. **Confidence** – (in your own voice – simply because it's yours . . .)
2. **Experience** – (let your experience shine and enrich others)
3. **Sensible** – (what is the most sensible course of action? Are you using your time to the best of your ability?)
4. **Selective** – (use the right tool for the right moment, plug knowledge gaps where necessary, but avoid creating habits that are not necessary**)**

Elevate your skills and see your confidence grow!

Ironically, with all the digitalisation around us, we should actually feel more confident than ever before . . . confident in our humanness, confident in our uniqueness, confident in the value of our experience.

Indeed, as we see so many around us converging into 'robot speak' it is actually easier than ever before to stand-out *if we choose to and learn the skills outlined here.*

If we recognise and seize the opportunity this affords – we could be at our most powerful when it comes to written communication.

So **which4words** that spring to our mind here are:
1. **Opportunity** – (the time to stand out is now)
2. **Elevate** – (your skill set)
3. **Differentiate** – (don't be part of the crowd)
4. **Clarify** – (what's needed by all)

What would your Word Bank to summarise this chapter be?

For this chapter we could suggest a Word Bank as follows:

WORD BANK

Human Personal Voice Ownership Effort Engagement Expression Clarify
Stand-Out Differentiate Personality Embrace Confidence Thrive Context
Experience Pride Evaluation Challenge Verify Celebrate Elevate Hone

---

What might your Word Bank for this chapter be?

6 Taking others' Compasses into account

We've looked at written communication from a general perspective, as seen through your formative influences in childhood, through the lens of your Purpose and your Uniqueness.

But of course you don't exist in a bubble: your interface with the world, whether it be local or global, makes sure of that.

So this chapter is about understanding how to write effectively to others who may have a different Compass

How do you accommodate their communication needs alongside your own?

Maximise your outcomes by assessing your input as follows:

- The simple act of asking yourself who you are talking to and trying to look at their communication through their eyes can be a superpower
- It arms you with the emotional intelligence that human interaction yields
- What outcomes matter to them?
- How do I tailor my message to these people's expectations whilst still being me, and managing the outcomes I need?
- Which **which4words** prompts shall I choose, to kickstart me to results in the task in hand?

Start by being curious about other People's Compasses

We briefly introduced the notion of curiosity in the last chapter, as a trait that helps you personally learn new things and flourish.

Now you'll see how curiosity also helps you understand others. Ask questions, share insights, see things from their perspective, and balance this with yours. This will boost your chances of communication success.

Supportive environments foster both curiosity and learning

The answers you need can be easy to find once you start getting curious.

In your career you'll come across organisations of all types and sizes, and you'll deal with people at differing career levels, disciplines, generations, and cultures.

What are they likely to have in common? The need to deliver optimal business performance through effective writing. Ideally the desire to improve their personal career development as well. Effective coaching builds positivity. Effective writing follows from that. It's not about the red pen approach on mistakes made: it's about embracing getting it right.

So what could we suggest could help? Well first and foremost, the motivation has to come from each individual themselves. We've laid the foundation for this already, on the lines:

- Each will already have confidence that they're following *their Compass* on how to communicate well
- Each needs to be curious to find out how others communicate too
- Each needs to care about their personal and professional *development*

What can work wonders to raise awareness of what works for companies?
Companies often find this method can work wonders. How it works is this: ask people from differing departments and differing staff grades to form a 'communication discussion group' in the spirit *of sharing what they consider 'best practice.'*

The group can bring along anonymised samples of real-life writing to be used openly and positively as a discussion topic, looking at the following parameters:

- Were they clear?
- Were they inclusive?
- Was the tone right?
- Had they engaged?
- Did they lead to the right action?
- Were everybody's outcomes met?

And so on.

Companies can find this so helpful, and of course the individuals too, as long as it's handled positively. That is, never to lose sight of the exercise: to get a sense of 'the best bits' in each. Because everybody can produce 'best bits' in part – but effective writing produces 'best bits' throughout. And that's what this book has in mind for you!

These findings can become a great metric for all.

We know from experience that if the environment is supportive and inclusive, people can feel confident and positive enough to take ownership of some aspects of their writing that they see quite differently now. You might even find comments such as:

'That came over as gobbledegook! ' or
'Did I really write that? I sound quite rude!' or
'Oh I didn't mean that . . .'
'I could have set it out better'
'That did come over well. Well done . . .'
'What a useful technique'

'There's more to it than I'd realised. Thanks for the eye-opener'
'It's much easier to see how to write effectively now that we've talked it over'

What a breakthrough, what a lightbulb moment. Writing should indeed come over as:

1. **Clear**
2. **Personable** (even friendly where possible)
3. **Meaningful**
4. **Impactful**

And hey presto, we have here **which4words** that a group discussion was easily able to identify. Do try it in training events or breakout sessions that you attend. It works.

Reading things out aloud can help immensely
People really don't do this enough.

If it doesn't *sound right*, then it's probably not going to work as well as you hoped. This isn't just from your perspective – but from your readers' viewpoint too.

It can be as simple as that.

Personality affects the way others might write

We've looked at your personality previously, now we need to look at others' too.

When you interact with people around you, it's super important to understand your audience and tailor your communication style to suit. Volumes have been written about the importance of emotional intelligence in communication and there are countless systems for identifying personality types.

But that's not the remit of this book. No, we're looking at the basics here: how the simple act of asking yourself *who you are talking to* and *trying to look at your communications through their eyes* can truly be a superpower.

What is the Compass directing *their* communication? What have they identified as their chosen communication through life, as we discussed earlier in the book?

Naturally, context affects how you project your personality
Think about a typical day in your life. Can you think of 4 distinct types of individuals you might interact with?

You could start by writing down the first 4 groups of people that pop into mind. How about:

1. Friends
2. Family
3. Colleagues
4. External people you do business with

Now think about how and why you might interact with these groups. Would you write to each one the same way?

Let's look at a text message we might write to family:

"Hello Daddy dearest, watcha up to? Pls. pick me up at 8. Ta."

What do you notice about this example? It's familiarity? Informality? A certain tone that's unique to a specific relationship? Would you write this way to a restaurant to make a dinner reservation? To cancel an insurance contract?

Now let's look at an example of a more formal email – perhaps to your boss at work.

Hi Gary,

As we are approaching the end of the quarter I would like to find a one-hour slot with you and the other Directors for our quarterly steering committee meeting. Please let me know 2 or 3 slots that would suit you next week. I will coordinate with the others based on your inputs, and schedule accordingly.

We have a lot of exciting progress to show – and require a decision on our go live date.

Many thanks,

Kind regards,
Bart

Now imagine you were writing to your best friend to meet you at the pub tonight – would this formally structured communication be appropriate?

Looking at the workplace, what personality types can you identify?
Within a professional setting, identifying the individual personality type of those you are communicating with can help to get the right results.

Right now think of a typical day at the office. Are there distinct types of stakeholders you interact with? In a large company environment, we commonly see:
- Creative Types (Creative Marketers, Artists, Designers etc.)
- Analytical Types (Engineers, Accountants, Scientists, Coders etc.)
- Commercial Types (Commercial Marketers, Sales, Procurement, etc.)
- Support Staff (Administration, Back Office, etc.)

- The Trainers/Educators
- Clients/Customers

Consider how you might approach each one of these stakeholder groups – by thinking about what traits might have lead them to this function.

As a broad brushstroke, we may find clues as to their preferred communication styles:

Creative types – generally seem to be motivated by the 'Bigger Picture' – understanding a vision, a direction, a mood, a vibe. They can be less interested in all the nitty gritty details, the numbers or any 'superfluous' information not directly linked to their brief.

Analytical Types – can be highly motivated by details. Facts, figures, professionally researched arguments, context; things that can be set out in black and white. The more the better. They favour proof beyond a reasonable doubt. Fewer opinions, less conjecture. Actions. Outputs. Clarity. Their default writing style will be technical.

Commercial Types – tend to thrive when Clear Goals and Targets are set. What success looks like is something they like to define. Metrics. Resulting Rewards. Talking points/context to help create relevant strategies. So we see a slight crossover in writing style from technical to creative.

Support Staff – often the glue between functions, often excelling at interpersonal connections and communication. So interactions with them should often be personal and insightful. Maybe we could go as far as to say warm – showing an extra dollop of emotional intelligence (though everybody needs this to some degree of course!).

Of course the personality types will vary (as in each grouping we outline), but generally these are not as transactional as others, often preferring:
- being able to plan vs. being surprised
- as much context as possible to help them formulate the best plan of action as they see it
- collaboration not commands

The Trainers/Educators – as you would expect, their style is likely to be a composite of all the styles we've highlighted, and then some. They'll be aware of differing learning styles and the importance of matching communication to readers' expectations, as far as is feasible.

That's a helpful approach for us all, and there are easy ways we can pick up on this. Try to tune in to people's communication preferences.

For example:
- Some people will favour visuals so will like pictures, charts, and diagrams to help process information. They 'see' the picture – and can like the immediacy of TikTok, Instagram and YouTube (where we must point out the written captions matter too and have to get to the point in shorthand. A real skill!)
- Others may favour auditory, the sound of the words used, and this no doubt explains the rapid rise in the popularity of podcasts, which can also be revisited and processed at a time of people's choosing. That 'sounds right' to them
- Some will prefer kinaesthetic communication which, put simply, means they prefer to learn and provide information in the form of practical exercises or role-playing/imagining situations. This 'feels good' to them
- Others may prefer reading and written communication. This 'makes sense' to them

Clients/Customers – Here too you'll find a composite of styles, and you need to be super-focused to pick up on these. Your business goal must always be to write in such a way that you're providing a virtual handshake to pull people towards you, not a virtual 'don't-care-shrug' or even worse, a 'slap' that pushes them away**!**

Now here's a thought: hold a picture in your mind of each group and their preferred style.

You'll remember the modes more easily. And this hack works for all and can be a particular help for people who find writing challenging because of dyslexia or other neurodiverse writing challenges. It's a fun technique into the bargain!

As writing is such a major interface with the world, we have to get with the programme and by now you'll be seeing more clearly why effective business writing covers so many more angles than people often realise. It's a challenge to rise to, to be:
- Part enabler
- Part technical writer
- Part creative
- 100% professional and human

The strands need to come together not just for *your* Purpose and Compass but *others' too.*

There are also personalities you might label informally yourself!
There are of course other classifications out there for you to research, to guide you in the right direction to tweak your communication to work. Chances are you'll also formulate your own classifications!

We've all come across 'The Bore,' 'The Dragon,' 'The Bossy One' and so on. And so often these labels arise from how readers react to those people's business writing, not their spoken words. You'll find the gentlest-mannered people can seem to bark out orders in terse emails, so at odds with their general demeanour.

We'll be looking further into this, from a slightly different angle in Chapter 8 with examples. And we'll invite you to do some detective work of your own!

So it's good to realise it's best to take a step back from time to time and see how far your tone might need to adjust to the type.

Let's recap with which4words what you've learned so far about Others' Compasses

What words might you use to help you adapt your writing to suit those around you? What springs to mind so far? We could suggest:

1. **Observation**
2. **Selective**
3. **Tailored**
4. **Relatable**

The more we all continue to relate to those around us, the more we see how it turbo-charges the effectiveness of our business writing.

Also tailor your style to match cultural dynamics

Have you ever noticed or been exposed to cultural differences when you communicate with individuals from different countries? From our personal experience, living and working in multiple countries across continents, we can tell you that communication styles vary greatly. So we all need to develop what's termed *cultural intelligence.*

From the direct to the meandering

Whole books are dedicated to this subject. We'll just highlight some key pointers to help you tune in to and understand others' Compasses in this respect.

Cultures that tend towards a direct approach

Certain cultures tend to take a more straight-forward, structured, and literal approach to communications. You'll find a give-away in this sort of writing:

"This report is missing the point – please re-work it with a focus on my specific request" or "I have not heard anything from you for the past 3 weeks – have you done any work?".

They also see no problem in answering questions with the very direct 'Yes' or 'No' – unaware that other cultures might find this insensitive.

Whilst there's no bad will whatsoever behind such direct statements, they can end up being offensive to those not used to communicating in this way.

And let's look at it from their perspective too, when they receive what they consider 'fluffy' communication that meanders, that is, to their mind, goes off course.

This is communication displaying what they view as unnecessary 'fillers' that, in their opinion, dilute the message by not getting to the point. They can react negatively, feeling that this sort of writing is wasting their time/inefficient/'beating around the bush' by not getting straight to the heart of the matter.

Reserved versus expressive cultures

For many cultures, the concept of 'face' or more specifically 'saving face' in front of others is a particularly important cultural sensitivity for you to consider.

For example, if you were to provide constructive criticism, or express dissatisfaction with someone, it would be very prudent to write a targeted message directly to the individual in question, encouraging a one-on-one discussion – without copying in others.

To express such concerns in a public fashion could cause the individual 'to lose face' in front of their peers. It's not fair to put them in that position.

Even the way you frame questions can assist intercultural expectations

For example, in an intercultural group discussion some may prefer to say 'Yes' to a question posed because:
- they may not have fully understood you (which may be as basic as a language problem)
- they prefer to agree, rather than disagree openly with the group which they may feel will cause embarrassment to others, as well as to themselves
- they don't feel resilient enough to argue their case, even though they disagree

To deal with this, it's a good idea to check understanding before putting things to a vote, for example, and to make people feel comfortable that their opinion matters, whatever it is.

Open questions are likely to fare better than closed ones across cultures
Consider how the closed question:

Is your report ready? is likely to lead to a one-word reply 'Yes' or 'No.'

It's true that the one word 'Yes' would be fine but, in operational terms, 'No' leaves you wondering *'why not'*? And wondering *'when will the report be ready'*?

So in this case an open question:

'Can you tell me if your report is on track – and when you're able to send it? Thanks'

Is both strategic and performance-targeted, to secure that essential information.

And if a bit more of a nudge is required, something on the lines:

'I imagine your report is ready to send now – if not, let us know what we can do to help?'

can lead to the answers you're looking for.

AI may not cover cultural differences. Its output depends on input – which may only draw on the inputter's bias

As an interaction with AI can itself tell you:

'If the data used to train AI is not diverse, the AI will likely reflect those biases. This can lead to cultural insensitivity, as the AI may not understand or respect cultural nuances. For example, if an AI is trained mostly on Western data, it might not perform well in understanding Eastern cultural contexts.'

So bear this in mind: there are extra elements involved in communicating across borders, and globally. The human steer is needed!

'Passive translation' – one such instance of cultural bias
When foreign readers are using AI to auto-translate your business writing, distortions may creep in, without you even knowing. Forewarned is forearmed on this one, otherwise you could end up both puzzled and of course not getting the results you hoped for.

CASE STUDY – AI Processes may affect communication without you knowing
Many websites offer a click button facility so that visitors can view their content in multiple languages. It started off with viewers seeing a pre-written version of the content provided. Simple. Then services such as Google, began offering browser plugins that could translate website content in real time/on demand (with varying quality) – allowing the user to generally get the gist of the content, without focusing too much on accuracy.

Now, however, as AI background services try to integrate more seamlessly than ever, these processes may be happening automatically, without your knowledge.

We stumbled across one such case recently. A UK national, now resident in Germany, increasingly finds his digital life often becoming extra complicated. Why? Because he still has English accounts that become increasingly confused by Geolocation – because this shows he's not actually in the UK.

So what happens? Well, German sites tend to be confused by the English language settings of his computer . . . and the list goes on. But until fairly recently he was presented with either a clear error code as to what was going wrong, or simply a choice of what to do (display in German – or be redirected to the UK site, for example).

With the onset of 'seamless integration' this may no longer be so clear cut . . . as the following example shows.

When buying something from a German seller on an online auction platform in Germany, he messaged the seller (in German), to enquire about shipping status, as no progress was showing after a few days. A reply popped up in the app on his phone with a slightly incorrectly worded reply in English. Strange he thought – but perhaps the seller saw he had originally registered his account in the UK and was trying to be nice, or perhaps it was just a coincidence.

Either way he proceeded to reply in English, and they exchanged a few messages back and forth.

Later that evening when checking his emails, he noticed an email with a transcript of the conversation, which had been sent to his mail account, as per his account settings.

Now here's what greatly surprised him: the conversation had been transcribed as a jumbled mix of English and German. Digging deeper, the app on his phone had decided (because his phone settings are in English) to auto-translate the German messages for him.

He could only assume the same would have applied on the other end for the German user once he had switched to English. Confusing at best, misleading at worst.

This will happen increasingly so be prepared – and once again, as we suggest throughout, write in a way that is both helpful to the tools but also less ambiguous in its output.

Exercise

If you have to work in multiple languages, have a little play around with the translation tool of your choice. See what distortion you may find and discuss this point with others too.

It's best to be aware of what might be happening to your intended communication.

There's so much more to find out about diverse cultures' preferred communication styles, which we naturally can't fully cover within the remit of this book. So do your research: it'll pay rich dividends!

We suggest **which4words** here could be:

1. **Universal** – (think things through when you write, identifying simple messages and key concepts that are easily understood by as many as possible)
2. **Short** – (shorter messages are less likely to be interpreted or translated incorrectly)
3. **Supportive** – (make readers feel free to ask questions if anything's unclear)
4. **Awareness** – (be aware that the unexpected might become more of a regular occurrence as these 'seamless' tools become more widely deployed)

The Polite Conundrum

Thinking of others generally: What's polite, and what's not?

Sometimes we can gauge what will be the preferred politeness levels for people we're communicating with. Sometimes we have to start from a position of not knowing that. We might have to write to an individual unknown customer for example, or to a colleague that we haven't met in person, as just two examples. Let's look at some possibilities.

Cultures that default to politeness or quasi-politeness in their writing

Some cultures have an inbuilt focus on 'politeness' which can prove bewildering to others. Why? Their use of niceties, *please* and *thank you*, is straightforward enough. But there's also a tendency to express upbeat, complimentary, or *apparently complimentary* comments, even if that's not necessarily the focus of what's trying to be conveyed.

An example is *"Great inputs – let's build on that!"* which might have been the true meaning but also might have been meant as *"not really what I was looking for – try again."*

And when the words *"With respect"* precede a statement, it's almost certain that the rest of the sentence will mark disagreement with whatever the other person has proposed. Things may not be as they seem from the literal words used.

'Auto-pilot' politeness can also prove problematic

Sometimes what we might consider 'default' politeness might not really be politeness at all!

You know the sort of thing. You're experiencing a really difficult day, for whatever reason. Maybe you got into work late because of traffic problems. Maybe you're finding life just too hectic, and your workload is off the scale. Maybe a company's delay at dealing with a problem is costing you a fortune and you need a speedy resolution.

And the first email you open that day, from someone who knows you're having problems (and might even be from the company causing those problems!), starts with:

'I hope you are having a great day.'

Duh!

It's what we call auto-pilot politeness, and it really isn't great news.

And there are many comments on online discussion forums that seemingly polite phrases such as the following, can be taken as passive-aggressive on occasion:

'Happy to discuss if easier?'
'Just a friendly reminder I need your reply asap, please'
'We're sorry you feel that way about the service you received'

'Thanks for reaching out to us' (in reply to a complaint!)

What are your pet peeves? Have you ever discussed these with others? It's such a useful thing to do!

Another 'auto-pilot polite message' is this:

'I hope you are well and had a wonderful weekend.'

What do you think of this? On the one hand, it's a friendly message, seemingly forging a relationship with the receiver. But you soon suspect that if the person starts their email in a similar way every time, is it just a template? And therefore not personal at all? You begin to think: they're not really expecting a reply to this opener, are they? And if it's from your estate agent/realtor for example, who you've been chasing for weeks to expedite completion of a sale, maybe they should weigh up courtesy and time pressures, and cut to the chase?

It's good to be aware of this if you use these expressions. You might have meant well, but if people react badly, time to rework your message!

Sometimes even one or two words can work wonders

This is good news because it's easy to achieve. Just look at the following two extracts and we'll ask you a question afterwards.

Extract 1
Ben,
Please can you send your presentation across this week?
Regards
Sara

Extract 2
Hi Ben,
Please can you send your presentation across this week?
Kind regards
Sara

Did you spot any noticeable difference in tone in the extracts?

Possibly not. But most people feed back to us that they find Extract 1 'unfriendly' and Extract 2 the reverse. *And just two polite words made the difference.* They were 'Hi' and 'Kind.'

Build connections and develop relationships through your writing. It will serve you well.

And if you've done that, you'll soon tune in to others' styles. Beyond that, consider going one step further – and discuss with others what *they like to see* in written messages and what irritates them. Best to write to their preferences whenever possible, isn't it?

And even the curtest amongst us, might have the lightbulb moment that, when people sign off *'Kindest regards'* to them, it might be rather rude not to reply in the same way!

The clues are so often there, literally in front of our eyes. Take advantage of them.

Generational differences in communication style

AI is such a great help if we want to compare and contrast the writing styles of Boomers, Millennials, Gen Z or Y etc. There are extremely useful programs that imitate appropriate styles depending on which platform you want to tailor your messages to.

It's still helpful to have a fix on the terms yourself and not fall into the trap of pretending you're of the generation you're targeting. Authenticity matters. You can't just accept that *'no cap'* means *'not lying'* or *'bet'* signifies *'agree' in* 'standard English' as two fleeting examples. It's the very nature of changing Millennial or Gen Z or Gen Y styles that it's bad news if people outside their group try to imitate their style. Their natural reaction: let's move on to new expressions!

Indeed there'll always be an upcoming generation who will choose different slang, and different sentence construction. It's the nature of language evolution and it's arguably accelerating.

What we focus on here is the workplace challenge we all have: to know when to be 'standard' (and what that means) – and how and when to adapt, according to target audience/sector expectations.

A broad brushstroke look at generational differences in communication today
We're taking a brief foray in here, simply so you can tune in to what you might find is going on. But also realise that so much will soon change again!

A few words about emojis
A lot has been written on about emojis in the workplace. Online discussion forums highlight how the jury can be out as to whether they are a help or a hindrance. In fact there is an argument to be made about the positive effect for certain groups to use them as a tool to convey emotions, where traditional forms of communication might not allow them to (Talbot J.M., 2020).

But in an everyday business writing context, do people readily understand their meaning, especially when nuance is involved? And as the choice of emojis is ever-growing, the nuances can just get more and more confusing, even difficult to see quite apart from interpreting. And people from different generations or cultural backgrounds, and so on, might interpret emojis differently and so your message could be misunderstood.

For example, the peach might be innocently used as the hallmark emoji for Georgia in the US but might mean something very different outside this state. Very fortunately people are speaking up to tell businesses about this, and please do be aware too.

And people can use emojis, consciously or subconsciously, to signify *'if you don't understand this, you're not in our group/generation/clique'* and so on.

For example, even the much-used *'thumbs up'* emoji can imply a positive message within some cultures but negativity in others. For example, as widely reported on discussion forums, Gen Z can even consider it as passive aggressive. They can view it as a snub: a lazy and overall non-interactive communication, ending rather than fostering conversation.

So tread carefully with emojis as they can be an actual barrier to inclusivity and, beyond that, feedback often suggests they damage reader/customer perception of professionalism.

Once again know when to be 'standard' (and what that means) – and how and when to adapt, according to target audience/sector expectations.

In all cases, context matters – which takes us to the next point.

'Standard language' works best in many communication tasks

For example when communicating internally or with stakeholders covering multiple disciplines, and customers from differing areas, a consistent corporate style can give cohesion and pull everyone together, not separate them into sub-groups with their own language. This is best reserved for when we have specific sectors to target – in marketing and sales campaigns and social media posts, for example.

But outside these functions, standard language has a better chance of standing the test of time – that is, it can remain intelligible to most for longer.

So what is 'standard language'?

As far as English is concerned, in their Bite-sized Learning Series (BBC Bitesize, 2024), the BBC usefully explain the difference between Standard and Non-Standard English as follows:

> '**Standard English** is the form of English that is taught around the world and understood by all speakers of the language. It uses correct grammatical rules and can be thought of as the formal, official, or polite way of speaking or writing.
>
> **Non-standard English** is the informal version of the language, which can change depending on where it is being spoken. It contains lots of slang (very informal versions of standard words), which can be particular to a certain area or group of people, so may not be used or understood by everyone.'

Language evolves

That said, even standard language is evolving fast in the light of the digital age,

It's fascinating to look back in time at written communication in the workplace. Even in the last half century there's been an upsurge in change through the influence of younger generations.

It wasn't that long ago that upcoming generations entering the workplace adjusted, unquestioningly, to their managers' style of writing.

However alien and antiquated it might have seemed to them, they found themselves in the echo chamber of the time. For example, they enclosed attachments to their formal letters in the style of a previous era: *'Please find herewith a copy of the document requested'* (and, dare we say it, some professions carry on in this vein today!)

But now we're increasingly seeing the opposite. The newest entrants to today's workplace expect *to influence*. As digital natives, used to dizzying changes in communication channels and segmentation, they unquestionably can have a lot to teach their elders!

And it's great if companies react to this and acknowledge what upcoming generations bring to the table as part of their corporate onboarding. One particularly effective way to make people feel they want to stay, is to highlight and embrace what they contribute to an organisation's success.

It has to be a multi-way process we suggest: each generation pooling communication strengths and constantly evaluating what *effective* business writing looks like for you and for your readers.

Effective corporate writing needs to:
1. Be something that feels authentic to all (a tall order when you start to design it!)
2. Be accurate and professional
3. Hit the mark and achieve objectives, each and every time
4. Be open and transparent – and definitely mustn't mystify

And see how easily we can summarise this in **which4words** to help design it!
1. **Authentic**
2. **Professional**
3. **Goal-oriented**
4. **Transparent**

Punctuation and grammar evolves too

AI tools can be so helpful in advising us on punctuation and grammar as we write, processing how things 'are usually done.'

But new entrants to the workplace can bring new nuances that aren't yet mainstream. For some, a full stop/period in an email or text can signal 'end of conversation' to them, not simply the end of a sentence. They can be averse to using it precisely because they perceive it as rude, or passive aggressive at best.

And if there are no full stops/periods, out goes the use of upper-case letters at the start of the traditional sentence, and then more and more for proper nouns too. So we see nouns like 'Saturday,' or 'July' become 'saturday' and 'july.'

Upcoming generations can favour abbreviations, and playful language. So an email to colleagues might look as informal as this:

Subject: running late for meeting

hi all,
chronologically challenged here . . . up for putting our meeting back an hour? 11 not 10?

Lmk

thks
Tomas

While this style can work just fine with internal colleagues if managers agree to it, would it work for other stakeholders?

A very real challenge regarding the written word is that it is so often forwarded to others outside the immediate distribution list, without the writer being aware that this might happen. So maybe not everyone would understand *'lmk'* denotes 'let me know' as one very small detail. Maybe not everyone would accept that *'being chronologically challenged,'* although playfully expressed alliteration, is any justifiable excuse for running late in business, without explanation.

And if our writing enters the sphere of banter which it so easily does if we regard it as chatty conversation, we can easily lose the business focus we need. This can mean that messages can prove embarrassing, even litigious, when read by a more formal audience.

Informality still needs to be professional.

What is your organisation's views on this?

Accessibility considerations come into business writing

We've already touched on this in Chapter 1, around the subject of dyslexia and other neurodiverse approaches. You need to research this wide-ranging topic in some detail. It deserves that you afford it that degree of importance.

You need to understand the needs of others in the workplace who may have differing ways to approach their writing and yours. Those with dyspraxia for example, may need to factor in extra time to plan and write. Bosses need to be aware of this. And dyslexic people tell us how helpful it is when writing is structured into identifiable components such as:

1.   Clear headings
2.   A structured layout to follow
3.   Bullet points to break up text
4.   Maybe highlighting different points you are making in different colours

But take care before you choose red and green highlighting colours because colour blind people might not be able to distinguish the difference between them. Also avoid visual clutter that can make processing reading more difficult, especially for people with Irlen's syndrome.

And choose a font and type size that's as accessible as possible. Many accessibility guidelines suggest sans-serif fonts such as Arial are easier to process than serif fonts such as Times New Roman. Do your research because the physical attributes of your writing matter. Even certain backgrounds might work better for some. Having corporate guidelines in place is such a help on this count.

We'll refer further to Accessibility in Chapter 7.

Now consider what outcomes are others out to achieve?

On top of the type of individual you might be dealing with, and the culture that shaped them, the third factor to address is: *what are the outcomes your audience want to achieve when they communicate with you?* How do you tailor your business writing in this respect?

CASE STUDY – Chasing approval to place a Purchase Order
Let's take this example. Imagine you are chasing the approval you need to place a purchase order with an external supplier on a critical project you're working on.

Picture the scene: your project deadline is slipping – construction is behind schedule – but you have identified a cost-effective local supplier that has spare workforce who could quickly come to your aid and get the timeline back on track. But this can only happen if you're able to confirm your purchase intent within the next 24 hours (as they have another client bidding for the same resources).

You need the approval of three busy Directors – a Procurement Director, The Projects Director, and a Safety Director.

You might be tempted to fire off a single email to all three, of course marked as urgent, but understanding what outcome each stakeholder might be most interested in could make your life easier. *Let's look at their needs*, one by one:

1. A Procurement Director

   They will most likely focus on Cash Flow – and of course making sure their Payment Terms are being followed, usually all leading to a good price. A targeted email, with a clear subject heading and an introductory paragraph focusing on the need for an urgent approval but also covering fully relevant basics, seen at a glance, such as:

   > *'Procurement Terms Accepted*
   > *120 Days Payment*
   > *3 Suppliers Screened*
   > *40% below reference price'*

   might help to proactively answer *this specific stakeholder's main interests* before you ask for your desired outcome, that is, the approval you need.

2. The Safety Director

   They need to be reassured that any new supplier coming on board is aware of the company safety standards and will work accordingly, so as not to generate any new risks within the project.

   So again, targeted comms such as:

   > *'Critical Supplier Approval – All Safety Standards transmitted and committed to, immediate onboarding/ training to commence upon your approval – timeline critical'*

   can work wonders.

   It can be the shorthand that works for that person.

3. The Projects Director

   They usually focus on 2 main things:

   a. being on time and

   b. being on budget

So again, targeted comms, for example, opening with

'Urgent Timeline Risk Mitigation – short window to maintain critical path, safety/procurement procedures fulfilled, no negative budget impact – immediate decision required'

will cut through the noise and grab their attention.

Conclusion:

In each of these three cases:

1. The body of the rest of the communication can be identical, with the same main content/attachments
2. Thinking specifically about the focus and desired outcome of your stakeholders can greatly streamline the efficiency of what *you* are trying to achieve

How to defuse conflict arising from others' differing Compasses

The early stages of setting up any group, be it for work (or even in a social setting), can be difficult when people are approaching from different angles. Let's look at a case study that shows how **which4words** can help!

CASE STUDY – Starting up a new venture

We know a team who, as we write, are in the process of trying to start-up their own consumer goods venture. They have brought together a group of four like-minded professionals to try and bring something new to the world.

After a relatively short 'honeymoon period' of between 2–3 months, the four people hadn't fully realised how important it would be to align their differing Compasses. Arguments started creeping in, emotions reared their head, and communication became increasingly difficult. We could even say the group was at risk of disbanding, simply on the basis of this ineffective communication.

Luckily, the group took a collective deep breath and resolved to look at the root cause of the misalignment.

One remembered a very helpful piece of work by a psychologist named Bruce Tuckman. Back in the 1960s he engaged in analysing group dynamics/behaviour (Tuckman, 1965).

Having observed and researched countless group situations, in 1965 Tuckman proposed a simple 4-step model on phases that groups go through, which he called *'Tuckman's Stages of Group Development'*. It can be paraphrased as follows:

1. **Forming** – group is polite, respects boundaries, treats each other as strangers, assigns roles

2. **Storming** – the group starts to push back against perceived leadership, boundaries are tested, emotions and conflict appear
3. **Norming** – differences are resolved – collaboration becomes effective
4. **Performing** – group reaches its maximum output

In 1977 he did add a further stage '**Adjourning**' – when team members are ready to leave and how the transition affects the group – but our focus here is how the group we're writing about adhered to the original four stages identified in 1965 (Tuckman and Jensen, 1977).

The group followed these **which4words: Forming, Storming, Norming** and **Performing** and collectively defused any conflict, knowing that what they were feeling was normal. By pushing through they could see that the best was yet to come.

It only took about five minutes of discussion to get to this breakthrough realisation.

What a great example of how to convey complex information and align people's personal Compasses with a 'Group Compass' using the power of these **which4words**.

Some principles stay relevant over time.

Cultural Intelligence

In a world where we target specific segments for our marketing reach, it's easy to forget that an abundance of our written communication is for mixed audiences globally.

Mindful of what you've just read, continue to keep an open mind, and consider:
- the need to simplify your messages to make them universally understood in a mixed audience
- how to get the tone right
- how to gauge whether the culture is individual or consensus-driven
- avoiding misunderstandings, such as not realising that some cultures or neurodiverse people might find it easier to say 'yes' or 'maybe' . . . . even when they mean 'no'
- how to tailor your writing when you know it's entirely aimed at non-native readers

We've found it so beneficial to run short workshops highlighting this to staff. The sighs of relief and comments at the end of these eye openers are such a bonus to all. Typical comments are:

'Oh that's why Henk seemed so abrupt in all his emails' or
'Oh that's why Sakura held back in the meeting' or
'Oh that's why Prakesh couldn't give us the ok right there and then to act on that'

Impactful and effective business writing in international trade

If you work in teams involved in this type of communication, it will help all if some-one oversees the ultimate success of the task. Consider the following:
- As ever, be professional
- Open doors at the same time through empathy of others' cultural communication styles
- Afford the courtesy, as well as the necessity, of tailoring communication as a result
- Delivering clear messages that people can understand
- Actively check there are no misunderstandings along the way, on both sides
- Keeping everyone informed, in the loop and ideally feeling valued as an integral part of success

Draw the strands together to craft the best solutions

Understand Others' viewpoints and Compasses but still be mindful of yours and how to craft the best solutions. That's the essence of effective, impactful business writing.

Don't be swept away by the tide of incessant communication from others and lose your identity or your ability to tune in to others' needs too. Both strands are part of your unique human advantage that you've so carefully been developing . . . and your sense of perspective on how to make the best sense of it all and evaluate the best way forward.

A **which4words** summary could be:
1. **Cultural-awareness** – (think of others' viewpoints)
2. **Empathy** – (develop rapport)
3. **Perspective** – (how to balance other's viewpoints/objectives with your own goals)
4. **Clarity** – (read between the lines/avoid misunderstandings using your advantage as a human)

What would your Word Bank to summarise this chapter be?

For this chapter we could suggest a Word Bank as follows:

WORD BANK

Reflection   Discovery   Engaging   Communicating   Influencing   Adapting
Tailoring   Evolving   Inclusion   Understanding   Aptitude   Personality
Culture   Awareness   Expectation   Unbiased   Measured   Authenticity
Accessible   Intelligent   Impactful   Relationship   Human   Courteous   Reciprocal

---

What would your Word Bank be here?

7 A broader toolkit to level up your business writing

By now you'll be fully attuned to the **which4words** approach to personalising the prompts that work best to kickstart you to success in your writing tasks.

But there are many more hacks, tips and tricks that can equally become tools in your toolkit to make your business writing the most effective, efficient and impactful it can be. We have gathered a collection of approaches that can help you to build even more momentum.

Now that you understand the **which4words** approach, this chapter is about:
- Showing you other fundamental writing tools to improve your business writing skills
- Understanding how becoming more comprehensive in your style/approach can unlock results
- Showing how the use of dynamics such as storytelling, can help us break through to the highest levels of engagement with our audiences

---

You're already mastering techniques and building confidence

As you're seeing for yourself, effective writing never happens by chance. We've given pointers along the way but it's your effort and your commitment that's brought you this far. *You* have developed your understanding of the importance of:
- The written word in communication
- Where your communication journey begins, from childhood on
- Your uniqueness as a human in a digital and increasingly AI world
- Understanding your Purpose
- Setting your Compass (and resetting as necessary)
- Understanding how to tailor your writing in view of Others' Compasses too (with all this entails)

So now that you're savvy with the **which4words** method, let's go a step further and help you with important business writing fundamentals and a number of further approaches and tools that can help.

Approach 1 – Fundamentals: be systematic about your writing

All writing needs to be right, clear, impactful and reader focused. We scatter many examples of writing that works throughout the book, and here we thought we'd just sum up some key points for you to routinely ask yourself.

Routine questions you now could be asking yourself

For optimal results, ask yourself some of the questions before you write, some while you write – and some after you've written!

How do you check what's right about your writing?
– Identify *your Purpose* in writing, otherwise how can you write the right message?
– Check for mistakes
– Check if the writing task is right for your bandwidth. By this we mean, flag it up if you don't have the time, resources, or energy to deal with a mountain of messaging. Best to discuss the problem at source with your manager, as problems don't go away if demands are too taxing. Many of the problems of information overload are about ineffective writing by others. But sometimes they occur because of a bandwidth problem
– That point dealt with, make sure you're writing to the right people at the right time
– Make sure you're communicating in the right medium/on the right channel
– Understand your brief at every turn, question and confirm as necessary

How do you make your writing clear?
– Get to the point in conveying your core message (but not at the cost of losing context – or losing rapport)
– Use accessible language. People need to understand it!
– Also use accessible fonts/backgrounds/colours/formatting for readability
– Edit well: it's a skill that pays dividends. Write what matters
– Confirm that people have understood, so that you get a firm understanding of what being clear involves, every time

How do you make your writing impactful?

- Use your power to choose words that cut through the noise!
- Even consider thinking like you would on social media. You readily understand the role there that key words and hashtags play in grabbing attention
- Use what you have learned in the book so far, about developing both your creative and technical writing skills
- Write to captivate the imagination of your readers
- Enjoy painting a picture with vivid adjectives and engaging verbs, maybe telling a story/anecdote of interest
- Create opportunities! For example by learning how to attach emotion, even drama to your core presentation

How do you make your writing even more reader-focused?

- Understand *your audience's* likely Compass and Purpose – and *how you'll need to align this with what you would like* readers to take away from your message
- Go one step further and ask the question from your reader's point of view: *'What's in it for me?'*
- Intentionally use words/written conventions that resonate with your audience
- Provide context as necessary, so people can make informed responses/decisions
- Empathise
- Develop rapport, build relationships
- Positive, proactive words help engagement and buy-in
- Continue to check understanding as necessary

A bit more detail to help

Effective writing results from a coordinated plan. A plan that avoids all those business writing bugbears that so irritate people. We listed many in Chapter 2, and you've also identified others for yourself in the last chapter.

Right? The further analysis to help

a) Make sure you identify *your* Purpose in order to write the right message. By now you've spent time and effort working out what your Purpose and Compass is, staking your place in the communication landscape, so don't lose sight of this. That's the first aspect of checking 'is my writing right?'

   Sometimes you will be the person instigating the task and the questions you pose may be predominantly to yourself. Sometimes you will be writing to a brief so at every turn, question not just yourself, but confirm with others too if necessary, that you are on track. You may (wrongly) feel this is taking unnecessary time – but as the saying goes *'It takes less time to do a thing right than to explain why you did it wrong.'*

b) As the individual who brings value to the organisation, you've also got to think about the specific *purpose of why you are writing* in each task you undertake. That's the second aspect you need to check: 'Is my writing right for what I am out to achieve?'

Helpful pointers can be 'Does this writing task require me to be:

Transactional? Providing information only? Relational? Empathetic? Highlighting an important update to team? Encouraging? Reassuring people of my professionalism, credibility, and trustworthiness? Influencing? Persuading?' The list goes on!

c) Your question 'Is it right?' also means you need to check that you haven't made mistakes and can verify what you're writing.

It's true that we are all likely to make punctuation and grammar mistakes from time to time. That's why using AI as our virtual writing assistant can be such a major help here.

The pitfall can be that, because we're generally so time-pressured, so inundated with information overload and so keen to empty our in-tray as far as humanly possible, it's quicker not to check. But as we pointed out in the first bullet in this section, that can lead to problems. And it's for that reason that one of the first things managers ask employees to do is *'please check before sending!'*

Messages riddled with mistakes do undermine credibility and professionalism, whether we think it fair or not. The reader has the power to make judgment. And do be aware that sometimes you will have to overrule AI's advice, because it can get it wrong, or doesn't know what suggestions to make. If in doubt, we suggest ask your manager or colleagues for help. Supportive work environments flourish.

d) The question 'Is it right?' also covers checking you're writing to the right people at the right time.

For example, how many times have you been puzzled as to why you've been included, or maybe excluded, from a group discussion or email thread? Or received an offer for a deal that expired the previous week, or invited to a meeting that took place yesterday? It happens and it's the definition of ineffective writing.

e) It also applies to doing your research. Which is the *right medium* for the message: for example email for rather more important, recordable decisions over instant messaging for more informal group discussions? Similarly, know which is the *right channel*. (More on this in Chapter 9).

Clear? The further analysis to help

a) The objective of being clear is to get to the point, but feasibly.

This means it mustn't be at the expense of losing context. Context is hugely important as recipients can need to know any relevant background in order to make an informed response. If there's a lot of back story they need to know, you could provide a link to further detail or provide a concise outline.

b) Getting to the point mustn't be at the expense of losing rapport.

- Too terse and people can be irritated (as we've shown earlier in the book)
- Don't for a minute think that ignoring things 'gets you to the point' faster! It doesn't – and it's also an irritant
- You may mistakenly think that firing off replies to the easy questions or the majority of questions, for example, is getting to the point. But you must also reply to the difficult ones/or the ones you feel too busy to reply to, as well!

c) 'Is my writing clear?' is also about researching accessibility requirements in your writing, as we also pointed out in Chapter 1 (when we first pick up on dyslexia and other approaches), and in Chapter 6. AI writing tools are a significant help here to keep you on track.

In outline, writing accessibly means you need to write clearly and concisely and with a well-structured layout so that readers, including those with visual, cognitive, motor impairments or other challenges, can access and understand what you write.

Do your research on this, as there are many factors to consider – for readability on screen or paper, for example, understanding where sans serif fonts will help, and providing text links for visuals. Even the colour/appearance of the background of your screen, or paper documents needs your attention. They can matter too.

Edit your content so key points stand out. Start with main points. Use AI where it will help.

d) Use plain language to reduce the risk of misunderstandings.

Also simplicity impresses: not only are you valuing other people's time, as well as your own. They deserve that don't they? And you come over as on top of your subject and your message is easier to buy into, as a result.

e) Over-embellishment can have the reverse effect, more easily seen as someone with muddled thinking, however unfair and far from the truth that might be. The days of verbosity and rarified vocabulary and unjustifiable jargon (meaning technical language used outside the group who will understand it) are over! It's no good coming over as pretending *'I'm cleverer than you'*: we all have an equal voice in communication today and that's a wonderful development.

f) Realise how helpful being consistent and clear is in the burgeoning use of AEO (Answer Engine Optimization). Writers now need to optimise content to answer AI question boxes so that these will surface easily and can be accessed and understood by bots.

By focusing on structured, clear answers, AEO can help a brand get featured in prominent spots like Google's featured snippets. Even in voice-based applications, a written script is likely to have been involved at the planning stage and be available for those with auditory challenges.

And consistency is emerging as a key metric that AEO looks for, to build brand awareness, credibility and ultimately, trust.

Impactful? The further analysis to help

a) Choosing words that cut through the noise can be a fun exercise.

Why use 'boring' words when you can engage better with words that are human-related and speak directly to the reader?

One of the most powerful words to do that is quite simply 'You.' Another is 'I' which fits in with our emphasis on identifying your Personal Compass. And another incredibly powerful word is 'We.' Impactful business messages will flip flop between the three words, ensuring they meld to build rapport and trust. They won't work without that skilful blend!

b) Beyond these, what are other powerful business words?

The words that will make impact for sure. What do you think? Ask your friends and colleagues too – it'll provide some interesting answers. We're sure you'll identify words such as these:

Results Easy Fast Cost-effective Now Reliable Objective Professional Yes Can-do Verifiable Sustainable Fair Green Eco-friendly Help Support Trust Credible Low-cost Premium Safe Quality Friendly At-your-service Today Guarantee Unmatchable Industry-Leaders Innovative Proven Secure Peace-of-mind Inclusive You're-Worth-It Value Creative Logical Objectives-focused World-class Diversity-ambassadors Consistent Dependable Community-focused Excellent

If you're not already choosing high impact words, do consider it now. What words can you tweak that would be right for the writing task in question? Make sure you can back them up!

c) The tips you have unearthed on layout, headings and bullets have the added bonus of making impact as well as enhancing clarity for the reader

d) An easy way to be impactful is to enjoy 'painting a picture' with your words. Add a splash of verve with vivid language.

This can be as easy as ditching the 'meh': a sign of indifference, boredom, or lack of enthusiasm – a vibe that you may not even realise you're putting over. Instead try to get into the habit not just of feeling positive wherever you can, but communicating positively too, wherever feasible. Here are some examples:

'Yes, that sounds great!'
'Imagine what success would look like. Let's go for it.'
'Yes, of course. I'll get on the case straightaway.'
'Certainly. Let's aim high on this one.'
'Well done team! Our pulling together worked wonders.'

This can really raise morale and be contagious.

e)   Telling a story or anecdote of interest can certainly create impact and also open up opportunities to put over your business message in a dynamic way. We're going to help you more with storytelling later in this chapter.

Reader-focused? The further analysis to help

a)   Have you worked out which is the right medium to use for the task in question? (There'll be more on this in Chapter 9)

b)   Are you assessing your organisation's writing as a whole, in this respect?
        Here's a useful example of this in action:

Network Rail, the company that maintains Britain's railways, has instructed staff to avoid using the word "passenger" in their communication with customers. The guidance, outlined in a 134-page document titled "Speaking Passenger", suggests using the more neutral term "you" instead. This is part of a broader effort to use less formal language and create a more welcoming and less frustrating experience for customers, especially during delays or cancellations (Neath, 2025).

So use what you are learning in this book to develop both your creative and technical writing skills, whatever your job role, to satisfy reader expectations.
    We'll explore this important theme next.

Approach 2 – Developing a comprehensive voice

The need 'to be many things' to our readers

Once you master a systematic approach, your communication path is so much easier to navigate throughout your entire career.

Success is an ongoing cycle, so let's elaborate on the introductory points we made in Chapter 1. We can a l need to extend our writing skills in a changing communication landscape, and consider how to be:

1. **Part enabler** – (write so that your readers know *what* to do, *when* to do it, from the starting point of *why* – all of which you will have set out!)
2. **Part technical writer** – (write clearly even when the subject is complex, so your messages work unambiguously, and readers don't have to 'decode' anything)
3. **Part creative writer** – in order to be impactful, engage and influence
4. **100% professional and human**

Let's look at each aspect now.

1 Why be 'Part Enabler' when you write?

Being an enabler starts with knowing:
- why you need to write
- how you need to write
- who you need to write to
- and who does what and when so you get the results you need

If you haven't got your mindset in place, it's probably better not to write at all, rather than waste your and others' time.

But get your mindset right, and hey presto, you're taking *accountability* for your words. You are enabling things to happen as you want them to, and it's a further marker of your uniqueness as a person.

Incidentally, it's a shame we sometimes see the word 'accountability' used in the workplace in a in a more negative way, around failure. That's not what we mean here. Being accountable for us means owning your words. You own them because you've actively and thoughtfully chosen them. They enable what you need to do: they make your communication effective in whatever writing task you're undertaking.

It's the core principle behind the **which4words** prompts that you are curating throughout the book.

2 Why be 'Part Technical' when you write?

Even if you're already a technical writer, or a student or professional working in STEM (Science, Technology, Engineering or Mathematics), do approach this section with fresh eyes. And if you're not adept at writing technically, do realise that increasingly we need to develop this skill.

For a start AI's LLMs (Large Language Models) use language not code. So although most of us aren't not coders by profession, we do need to write technically in the sense that our language is correct, concise, and unambiguous for AI as well as for our readers.

So how can you harness a technical approach?

Technical writing was a term historically used to describe a specialised type of writing for say, the scientific, engineering, medical, coders, IT or other technical users who need to receive specific guidelines and instructions etc.

At its best it's about refining complex information into simpler information for the reader.

So you can see the benefits for us all to have elements of technical writing in our workplace communication, where cutting through the noise is increasingly paramount. So ditch the waffle.

And to think like a technical person definitely involves looking out for mistakes. An eye for detail matters, just as it does for legal, healthcare and finance professionals who also fall broadly into this category.

They definitely expect writing that adds up, in every sense of the word. They know that there's a cost to ineffective messages that need rewriting for whatever reason, whether they mistake-riddled, or otherwise not right for purpose.

Avoid 'old-style' technical/legal/financial/medical/scientific writing etc.

That's why there has been such a noticeable drive to put even the weightiest of technical, legal, and financial documents etc into plain language: the language that people speak and more easily understand.

One word of warning about a style to avoid. Old style technical writing often utilised passive, not active writing – and to do so without thought can be a no in today's world. The passive form is a grammatical term where the subject in a sentence 'passively' receives the action, instead of doing it 'actively' themselves.

See how it works here:

1. *When any work is carried out in relation to any appliances, it's imperative the operative holds a relevant certificate of competence for each activity they elect to undertake.*

2. *In view of the regulations, the following calculation would need to be applied . . . (a calculation follows)*

Can you see why this writing can actually be unhelpful in the workplace and why the best technical writers (which you can be now!), will convert such text into the active form? We'll show you how this works, and why it's better.

Let's revisit example 1. In this case the instruction was specifically for engineers who would be using the instruction manual in question. We can rewrite it active form and in effect speak directly to the user in this way:

If you carry out any work in relation to any of the appliances, you must hold a certificate of competence for each activity you elect to undertake.

On similar lines we could also rewrite example 2 as:

In this case, the regulations do require you to do the following calculations . . .

So get your antennae out. Look out for passive forms of writing where you have to work out who does what and when. They can work if you really don't want the finger of blame pointing at someone: the passive can definitely hide accountability. That's a topic for discussion in its own right . . .

But in the vast majority of cases, ensure the active form does the work for you. Write clearly to your readers – no decoding required!

Of course there will be times when you'll have to offer more detail when the subject dictates it's needed. But you can help your readers by providing a link to the in-depth material or attaching a file with the extra information.

3 Why be 'Part Creative' when you write?

Some of us seem to be born creative! But if not, we can still work on writing creatively at work. In fact we need to, as part of our uniqueness as human and because of the fork in the road in terms of business communication today.

We may wish it could, but AI can't actually create content for us. Yes, it's brilliant at harnessing knowledge for us. It curates pointers that can help us achieve our objectives. But so far, it's always checking with us: 'Is that what you were looking for?'

So here's good news. As you saw in Chapter 1 there's likely be some childhood creativity lurking in all of us. The challenge is to unearth it, as it's been ignored as a general resource in the workplace for far too long. It's been relegated to a talent expected of dedicated marketing and advertising teams and the like.

Easy to see why, in the past, other teams in an organisation didn't even try to think creatively: 'it wasn't their job.'

But now there's a fork in the road. Business writing is a principal interface with the world and suddenly creativity is a much sought after commodity. Be your own person, have your own identity, get the spotlight on you and your organisation, and cut through the noise!

So how can you harness a creative approach?
When we explained Step 3 on our 4-step writing system, we promised we'd help you further on this.

Impact will help you write creatively
We know how AI looks at the big data, at what's already out there. To make a difference, to stand apart from the rest, use your human uniqueness to draw on the rich tapestry of language to make impact.

Can you break away from the norm? It does of course depend on the leeway your organisation allows. But you're most likely to have, or to create opportunities to make suggestions, and make your mark uniquely.

Don't be daunted. Impact can start with the simplest of changes. When we ask people what writing by others have made the most impact in the last week, the answer can be something so simple yet so effective. An example was a highly original out of office email reply, on the lines:

Dear sender
Thank you for your email . . . I'm out of the office due to . . .
Business Event, Vacation, Sickness, Meeting, Business Trip, Bank Holiday
I'll be back in the office on . . .
Best wishes

Each possibility had a relevant icon or emoji beside it, plus a box in which to place a tick as to which possibility applied. The autoreply ended by stating that *the email would not be read or answered in the meantime but giving contact details of other colleagues in emergencies.*

Why did this example immediately spring to someone's mind? It was because it was novel. They hadn't seen this before. The icons and emojis not only *grabbed* attention, but *focused* attention. That's a winning formula.

The visuals-added approach made the message more effective on many levels. We suggest it was because it was great shorthand, enabling the required response because:
– If you know that someone is out of office because they are sick, it affects how you will subsequently write to them.
– You won't feel angry if they haven't got back to your request last week, say
– It affords leeway – and you still know who to contact in that person's absence
– You also won't introduce your next message with 'I hope you had a good break'
– If on the other hand you know they have been on vacation, you can be friendly and hope they had a good time

Once again proof that effective writing results *in every case* from someone first thinking:

1. *'Why am I writing this?'* and
2. *'How can I get the right message over, so people know what's required?'*

The principles of effective writing remain refreshingly and encouragingly constant.

We can easily create impact by helpful formatting too, not just by the vocabulary we use. Interestingly, people are already voicing their annoyance at the standard formatting that AI routinely suggests. When we see the same patterns emerging all over the place, it becomes boring. Time to innovate and arrange things differently.

Exercise

What piece of writing has impressed you at work this week? Why was that? Make a note now. Is it a technique you could use more in your business writing?

Can you see how creating impact in how you present things can involve:

- *the look and feel, as well as*
- *the core content of what you write*

Approach 3 – The Magic of Storytelling

You can need to be a storyteller

We showed in Chapter 2 how the imagination and wonderment we show as children when we hear or read a great story is a formative influence – something to be treasured and nurtured throughout life. And yes, it can really help us in our careers where verbal literacy is such a sought-after skill.

Story telling as a concept will come more easily to some disciplines than to others. A friend who runs creative writing classes at a London Institute expressed surprise as to why she was increasingly seeing people from STEM (Science, Technology, Engineering, and Mathematics) backgrounds, and coders enrolling on her courses. Why was that, she mused?

The reason is clear to us: storytelling in a business context is no longer just for the natural-born creatives amongst us, such as marketers, as we'll explain.

Why is storytelling a useful business communication tool?

First and foremost, in line with the focus of this chapter, storytelling presents a great opportunity to showcase the uniqueness of you as a human. The most authentic storyline you can tell comes from within you. You just have to find it, and we plan to help you do that.

Here are just a few of the many other reasons why storytelling helps in a business context:

- People don't just buy in to products and services: they buy into people, and a story is communication clearly made 'human'
- And a well told narrative can put a person on their audience's radar so effectively. People can often find they tune in more easily to it than just to hard facts and figures or other information, and remember all of these things better when you embed them in a well-crafted storyline
- They can be more open to what the storyteller is suggesting, and in a business context there is likely to be an element of persuasion so that the narrative leads somewhere

But the very notion of storytelling can faze many people. How do you set about doing it? So let's help in this chapter. In business it can be simpler than you may think.

Core themes can help you develop a storyline

Even if you're not a natural creative, what you've just read should help you on your way. Once again refer back to your childhood imagination if you can. Even if dormant, there's likely to be something there!

Draw it out now. What were the great stories you may have read or heard in your childhood, or recently?

No matter how complicated, successful stories tend to be crafted around a simple core theme, for example:

- good versus evil, or
- triumph over adversity, or
- appearances can be deceptive, or
- human connection (or disconnection!)
- adventures and things learned, and so on

We've refined the list to core themes that could work in a business setting as they have a distinctive human angle that can engage your target audience. Do add some more now that could work for you. Let your creative juices flow!

Adding creativity brings the human touch to even 'technical' writing tasks

Here's an imaginary scenario to highlight how pooling resources can reap great dividends in our business writing. See how the sum of the parts can be greater than the individual inputs, when our business writing keeps a keen focus on the fuller picture. Let's dig deeper.

CASE STUDY – Planning a visit to an Engineering Plant

The following scenario is based on what might happen at a multinational and world-class engineering company, keen to show they play an active role in the local community.

Imagine that this year, they've decided to invite a small group of final year secondary school students to attend a two-hour visit to the company's Plant. So the company has appointed a small working group with delegates from different departments, to meet and decide on the programme for the students.

The group comprised two representatives from the engineering department, one from HR, one from marketing.

The engineers proposed a classic approach to the task, suggesting the visit be organised on these lines:

1. The company name and site location
2. ID needed
3. Time to check in
4. Where to assemble for check in
5. Safety arrangements (including hard hats to be worn)
6. Who's involved in the tour
7. The schedule: what you will see during the site visit
8. Departure arrangements

Yes, agreed the HR representative, you're right, these points need to be covered. But something's blatantly missing: *Why* is the visit happening?

And here we see an energising shift in perspective – an opportunity to change 'the mundane,' the patently correct, though rather boring initial approach. It's developing into something more interesting for the target audience, that is, the students. Shouldn't the visit cover *future opportunity for them,* as well as being *a pipeline for future recruitment* for the company?

Now the marketing representative stepped up. Let's inject some vitality they suggested. Let's make it more fun for the students. So let's write into the schedule time for refreshments at the end, and some marketing merchandise as takeaways. Something that friends and family would also get to see. That way the whole message about the event could be disseminated to the wider community, not just to the group of twenty students on the day.

So the point of this exercise is to show you how to plan your writing on the basis: what are the *overall* goals in any particular task? In this case:

1. *Is it just about the visit running smoothly, essential though this is?*
2. *Or is it just as much about 'How do you stand apart?' in your communication?*
3. *And what's your and your organisation's proposition? What do you need out of it?*
4. *This should be giving you a buzz – and transmitting this to others, to entice people to hear what you're saying, and get on board*

And if that buzz is missing, it's a key indicator that something's awry and needs fixing, one way or another.

Now you see how the power of clear technical writing added to creativity in your writing, takes the task away from *'I'm writing this because someone has asked me'* to *'How can we design a great piece of technical and creative writing to put the organisation on the map?'*

And this is what they then produced with identified staff responsible for each element:

Finalised plan for the site visit
1. The company name and site location
2. ID needed
3. Time to check in
4. Where to assemble for check in
5. Safety arrangements (including hard hats to be worn)
6. Who's involved in the tour
7. The schedule: what you will see during the site visit
8. Hospitality phase
   a. Refreshments
   b. Recruitment opportunities
   c. Key company messages and take away marketing merchandise
9. Departure arrangements

So let's analyse the development to the finished product: the site visit that went ahead.
1. The fact that there were people from differing departments got people *curious* and the group owned the revised plan through *consensus*
2. *Conversation* was the human driving force that yielded the written solution sent out to all involved
3. What's really fascinating in these sorts of exercise that do exist in the real world, was how the differing disciplines pooled their singular expertise into a *supportive group dynamic,* each learning from the others, and producing an 'approved masterplan'

4. The group could see for themselves that creativity (being open to new ideas) was the driver that showed them that *adapting* could be an effective way to solve a problem
5. They themselves had produced a whole storyline – which they owned – without even knowing it! They might indeed have been daunted if asked to do this at the outset!

Yet what a key transferable skill they demonstrated, and it's one that employers crave.

We could suggest **which4words** here as:

1. **Administration** – (the event has to be organised to run smoothly)
2. **Placement** – (we're setting out the reasons why we're a world class company)
3. **Proposition** – (we want to inspire as part of a community initiative and a recruitment tool. We are buzzing to show you why we're a great company *to work for*)
4. **Pride** – (we're proud of our values/our talent/our success – which makes us communicate with enthusiasm and fun, where the occasion permits)

Exercise

Have you any training workshops coming up? If not devise a mini one yourself. Get your boss involved in this one if you can.

Have a look at some recent reports or other written documentation you've seen. Invite colleagues from different departments to join you, in having a go yourselves in making the text punchier, with broader perspective. Add some active verbs and more dynamic adjectives and adverbs and you're on your way to becoming a storyteller! It can be as easy as that.

Story telling can also help you keep things on track

Have you ever left a presentation, or a long discussion frustrated that your audience seemed to totally miss the point of what you were trying to convey? Have you ever had a meeting that you thought was going to focus on a positive achievement – but unexpectedly turned into a car crash as people focused on something totally different? It's something politicians face daily!

Storytelling can be a great way of creating, sticking to and engaging others around a common theme or narrative of your choosing. And if things take an unexpected turn, it can help to bring the discussion back on track. Certainly back to the message you are trying to convey.

So just think up the core theme to the story you could write to serve your purpose in a business context. Imagine you're preparing a Quarterly Steering Committee for a group of senior stakeholders. The purpose? To update the status of a major project due to complete in six months' time. The current budget is projected to be 10% overspend and the latest estimate for the project completion date is 4 weeks behind schedule.

It would be very simple, when making a report or a presentation, to focus in a matter-of-fact way on these apparent stumbling blocks. Then this would be the main takeaway, and the senior stakeholders would walk away with an uneasy feeling about the project and its leadership, and of course you.

What if there was more to it that those headlines or a first glance might suggest?

What if there's a deeper level to explore – a new storyline emerging?

Imagine that, as the project lead, you had felt bad about the potential risks/delays/overspends (all of which were reported to the previous steering committee meeting), but since then:

- you could see that the many new processes and structures now implemented to get this project under control, had just started generating momentum over the last 14 days, and
- more project actions from the action list had been closed out in the last 7 days than in previous 3 months combined

That's *good news,* isn't it?

The story we would tell in this case would be a story about Momentum. About Turnaround. About hopeful triumph over adversity.

We would paint a picture of:

- where we were, and why
- what we changed, and how
- the results and momentum that change had led to

We'd then encourage the group to think about what the next steering committee might look like, based on the likelihood of continuing improved results.

We'd definitely resist the urge to hide, gloss over or indeed polish any of the facts, but would construct a well-informed narrative about the status of the project as you see it. Experience shows this will invariably lead to healthier, more engaging discussions with other stakeholders. Not only will you boost your confidence in finding your own story to tell – but it will also serve as an immensely helpful **compass** to refer back to, whenever the discussions may start to go off track.

Approach 4 – Be 100% professional and human

Being 100% professional is a concept that we're helping you achieve throughout. Don't lose sight of how this can set you apart for all the right reasons.

Writing as a human will also be becoming second nature to you by now, and we'll take the opportunity to give further tips along the way.

Choosing active verbs can help

Just as you saw earlier examples of passive writing in technical writing, this style does creep into general workplace parlance too. And it shouldn't! An example is:

It was decided that a more direct line of action could be advantageous.

If we put this into the active form, we know who did what. The passive form doesn't indicate this at all. And the active form it makes it more likely that the rest of the sentence will be more dynamic too. Let's have a go:

We decided that the company would reap a real advantage if we acted promptly and directly.

Introducing 'We' makes the text inclusive at a stroke as well: always a good idea in business communication.

Here's another example of a passive style which we'll now look at through an emotional intelligence and creative lens:

It became apparent that the division had outperformed the market in the current quarter and all stakeholders are to be informed in due course.

How do you think this could be made more active and dynamic, without altering any of the facts? Here's a suggestion:

Great news! Well done all: we've outperformed the market this quarter.

This also delivers an inclusive human connection, an important feature in storytelling. And people are always going to appreciate congratulatory wording. It's true that sometimes results may not be so good, but we can all choose to vitalise our words and offer encouragement.

The vocabulary *you choose* matters: don't overlook this word power you have.

Vibrant words help too

Once we're in the habit of using active verbs, we can find it easier to build in positive words that continue to foster *the emotional buy-in* we hope for in our readers. With so much information around, we need to make our words compelling, as far as we can.

So think about the sort of words that are likely to help. What words you like people to write to you? There will be answers there. That something's really going to help? That there's an unmissable advantage to be gained? Congratulations for your hard work? Thanks to everyone's efforts the Group is thriving?

Enthusiasm is contagious – never forget that. It can be such an under-used resource. We all need a lift at times, don't we? And it doesn't have to 'over the top' but it does need to be sincere. People don't like insincerity. They see through it.

Even something as simple as swapping 'nice' for 'great' could be a start. Or tweaking 'Targets met this month' to 'Great news: all targets met this month. Well done all' on the lines we outlined just now.

A pattern emerges if you look for it. Words such as the following can be the springboard to get people on board:

You We Now Save Free Advantageous Imagine Celebrate Let's go for it Thrive Exciting This will work Trust Yes Please Thank you Support Help

So don't be overly subdued. People don't engage with subdued writing any more than they do with over effusive writing. Have the confidence to promote your messages; to make a difference.

Positive impact isn't just about getting noticed. It's writing that can link to emotional intelligence too, both of which can inspire change, where companies might need to change procedures for example.

Exercise

What words occur to you right here right now as a springboard to help? You have the unique power to choose the right words yourself. Use it. What words could you perhaps be using more to make your written messages more vibrant?

For us, a recap of the chapter could be:

1. **Foundation** – (going back to basics can help to lay the foundation for great business writing)
2. **Universal** – (understand different types of writing to connect with the audience, whoever they are)
3. **Engaging** – (use writing as a tool to captivate, thrill, excite, not just explain)
4. **Evolve** – (try, learn, adapt, try again, – with so many tools at your disposal – your writing is a journey, not simply a moment in time)

What would your Word Bank to summarise this chapter be?

For this chapter we could suggest a Word Bank as follows:

WORD BANK

Toolkit Inputs Outputs Impact Mastery Confidence Clarity Evolve Variety
Useful Accuracy Engaging Comprehensive Adapt Dynamic Planning
Original Straightforward Imaginative Captivate Stimulating Journey
Pleasantries

What might your Word Bank for this chapter be?

8 Extra tips on Common Writing Tasks

You are now fully versed in the **which4words** method, applied to a well-rounded approach to business writing in general. There are, however, specific applications or areas of business writing that may require an even more tailored approach. Certain tasks lend themselves to certain formats, others have specific do's and don'ts, so let's look at some of the more frequent examples together and share some thoughts, tips and tricks that may help you master the ones you use.

So this chapter offers further points on how you can add the finishing touch that differentiates you as the 100% professional and human communicator you aspire to be.

For ease of reference, we class the common writing tasks we cover here in alphabetical order.

Calls to action (CTAs)

We have touched on calls to action earlier in the book, in regard to everyday business writing tasks, where it's important that when we write we know how to get to the point, but also how to engage the disinterested, not just those who want to know more. Clear CTAs can help all. This is as important an objective today as it was 20 years ago, and no doubt will be in another 20 years!

In general terms then, calls to action can ensure that those we communicate with know:
- what they have to do
- how, and
- when

But now let's address how useful a call to action can be in social media, as another tool in the successful writer's toolbox.

A call to action in social media is an invitation – or stronger exhortation – for the reader to engage with your content. It's intended to shift the dynamic – from a potentially passive, even indifferent reaction, to one of active engagement.

This can be as basic as actively requesting feedback or input in the form of an email, right through to rewarding a consumer – for example through the use of a competition on social media. A call to action can be anything that actively challenges the audience to get involved.

© 2026 Walter de Gruyter GmbH, Berlin | https://doi.org/10.1515/9783112217696-009

Research suggests that using a call to action (CTA) over standard passive text can result in 100–200% conversion uplift. This results in higher revenue generation (Sender.net, 2025).

What do calls to action look like?

You will have seen countless standard examples such as:
- *Sign up to unlock . . .*
- *Tag friends to enter our prize draw*
- *Start your 7-day free trial now*

And examples with added urgency, to make readers more likely to 'act now to avoid a fear of missing out' (FOMO). These could be on the lines:
- *Sign up in the next 48 hours to receive a free introductory course*
- *Subscribe today for a one-off 15% discount*
- *Hurry, stocks are running low!*

These sentences are likely to increase the interaction desired.

Other benefits that calls to actions can bring

1) Positive dialogue with your consumers offers immediate benefits. And there's another plus too: interaction helps to elevate your visibility and ranking within the various search algorithms, helping to further boost your reach. The gift that keeps on giving.
2) CTAs can also play a key role in building a community.

CASE STUDY – Starbucks' customer feedback initiatives

Starbucks, the American multinational chain of coffeehouses (as studied in detail by the likes of (Braineet, 2024), (Blankboard Studio, 2025):
1. Starbucks run frequent customer feedback initiatives involving CTAs
2. For example, they encourage customers to *"drop their comments below"* to provide feedback of their experiences, as a signal that they care
3. They also seek input for new product creations, clearly valuing their customers by so doing

4. They encourage other creative inputs – through, for example, their #RedCup-Contest via social media where they encourage users to show off their cup designs. In that sense, everyone's a winner – a positive, fun experience for all

Over to you! Tips to help you think creatively around CTAs

Tips you have gleaned throughout the book will have sharpened your imagination and highlighted the value of your human creativity, characteristics that pay real dividends when it comes to creating calls to action. You have the best chance of success by seeing things through your readers' eyes whilst at the same time 'grabbing their eyeballs' with words that make impact for the right reasons for the audience!

So, it makes sense that the tips marketers use can help you too! Let's reinforce the messages now:

- Use active words such as *Share, click, subscribe, sign-up, send, comment* etc.
- Personalise and involve: *Create my account, tag your friends, give me a 15% discount*
- Create Urgency – *Limited time offer, next 48 hours, today only, hurry*
- Create Intrigue – *Be the first to hear about our new launch; something bold is on the horizon*
- Consider setting up a storyline *(our suggestions in Chapter 7 can help)*
- Think up a Reward – for example, *Tag 5 friends to enter our prize draw; Sign up to receive 7 days free access!*
- Encourage feedback, especially if it focuses on inclusivity and a sense of 'Oh yes, I can identify' in the mind of the reader. Accordingly, you might write: *If you recognise this issue – sign up here; Share your ideas for our next release*

CV/Resumé Writing

One of the most critical yet also controversial areas in business writing today concerns CVs or resumés as they're also known. The good news is that there are many resources online that you can research to help you with structure – such as ideal length, key sub-headings, omitting personal data, simplified formatting and so on. But what we want to draw your attention to in this book, is how important it is to show the human touch, perhaps more than in any other application.

The CV is after all a snapshot of you, not of anyone else. We could echo the words of Oscar Wilde, in a famous quote widely attributed to him on exploring identity: "Be yourself; everyone else is already taken".

Research suggests a dramatic increase in the use of AI to auto-generate CVs for job applications (Onrec, 2025). This has unsurprisingly led to recruiters increasingly voicing their frustration at the generic, impersonal CVs landing on their desks.

Ironically, recruiters themselves are turning to AI tools to identify and sift out AI generated CVs – and so a figurative 'arms race' has erupted (Rio S., 2025), to try and find the few remaining candidates who invest the time to write themselves and who are genuinely motivated and qualified for the job in question.

Due to the sheer volume of guides, how to's and general text there is out there, on using AI to write CVs, the question of 'how to stand out' is likely to be a frequent one. Again ironically, this can lead to many auto-generated CVs looking remarkably similar.

So what are some of the reasons AI generated CVs don't quite make the grade? Well they come over as noticeably similar through what's clearly a generic formulation. They can come over as clinical notes. Where's the person there? Where's the personality?

This 'clinical' approach can manifest in:

- an over-embellishment of certain achievements which candidates can't explain or provide evidence for when they get to interview stage
- vague statements e.g. 'improved results' without providing context or detail

So it's not just the words on the CV recruiters are complaining about, it's also often about this lack of personal effort and interaction. It can act as a red flag from a cultural fit perspective. It can even raise issues on trust and honesty or motivation and work ethic.

Let's look together at an example of an auto-generated CV:

John Doe Email: johndoe@email.com | Phone: 555-1234

Professional Summary *Results-driven professional with strong communication and organizational skills. Seeking to leverage diverse experience to fill the open position at your esteemed organization.*

Skills
- *Detail-oriented*
- *Hard-working*
- *Professional attitude*
- *Dynamic thinker*
- *Strong team player*
- *Fast learner*

Experience
> ***Sales Associate, ABC Corp*** *(2021–present)*
– *Achieved high sales numbers as a professional team member.*
– *Collaborated with colleagues to meet organizational goals.*
– *Maintained high-quality standards in customer service.*

Marketing Intern, XYZ Agency *(2020– 2021)*
– *Assisted marketing professionals in creating campaigns.*
– *Demonstrated strong working relationships with professionals.*
– *Supported the team with organizational tasks.*

Education *Bachelor of Business Administration, Generic University (2016– 2020)*

Additional Information *References available upon request.*

What strikes you after reading this clearly auto-generated example CV?

Is it engaging? Does it have the personal touch? Imagine you are a recruiter: would you be excited to meet this individual?

But fear not, to truly stand out, this is a perfect task for the **which4words** system! Let's think about how to apply it after you've read this example of a job posting:

Job Title: Digital Marketing Specialist
Are you passionate about digital innovation and eager to make an impact? We are seeking a creative and data-driven Digital Marketing Specialist to join our team. In this role, you will be instrumental in transforming our online presence by designing and executing cutting-edge digital campaigns that engage and grow our audience.

What You'll Do:
– *Develop and implement innovative digital marketing strategies across social media, SEO, email, and paid ads*
– *Analyse campaign performance using data-driven insights to optimize results*
– *Collaborate with creative and product teams to deliver compelling content and user experiences*
– *Stay ahead of industry trends and emerging technologies to keep our brand at the forefront*

Who You Are:
– *Experienced in digital marketing with a strong understanding of the latest tools and platforms*

– Analytical mindset with the ability to translate data into actionable tactics
– A collaborative team player with excellent communication skills
– Excited about experimenting with new ideas to challenge the status quo

Join us and help shape the future of our brand's digital storytelling and growth!

So how can we personalise our CV to the task? Let's first summarize our understanding of the job requirements – both from a candidate as well as a role point of view (POV), using the **which4words** approach. What would be your main takeaways?

A *general summary*, using **which4words** in this way, could be:

1. **Experience** – (relevant experience in the field is essential)
2. **Analytical** – (a technical component is required, not simply administrative)
3. **Innovative** – (prepared to try new things and change the way things are currently done)
4. **Communication** – (good at collaborating/communicating with others to work as part of a team)

With a clear understanding of what the role demands and what the recruiter is looking for, *we understand what we need to project clearly in our CV* to demonstrate a fit for this role. So we could distil into **which4words** the summary that *we could use to personalise* and structure our CV to suit. With the role in mind we might use the following:

1. **Qualified** – both academic as well as professional/practical experience can be demonstrated within the desired scope of the role. Adept at leveraging data insights to optimize campaigns and solve marketing challenges whatever the scale
2. **Creative** – full of ideas about potential innovative approaches/solutions to the problems the company is facing. We're inquisitive and a go-getter
3. **Sociable** – we thrive in social environments and understand that collaboration with others is the key to success/progress. We're known to be fantastic to work with
4. **Learning** – as a critical thinker, we not only seek to uncover the hidden learnings in our daily work but are eager to continue to grow as an individual. It's something we recognise as an opportunity within and beyond this role

Additional Information might include our outside interests which highlight our personality and that essential human touch such as:

Fluent in English and German; volunteer social media manager for local charity organization; taking evening classes in the history of art

---

However you approach the challenge when it comes to writing your CV, just remember this: your personality, your uniqueness as a human, your drive, your motivation, your tone of voice – all of these need to shine through!

If a recruiter has gone to the trouble of actively looking for someone to join their team then that is exactly what they want: *someone*, not just another generic autoreply.

Emails

Let's cut to the chase: people continue to argue over the relevance or importance of emails in the current age. Many people try to avoid them at all costs, favouring simpler forms of communication such as voice notes or WhatsApp messages. But emails are clearly still flooding the workplace. What's important is to use them effectively, not to let them create problems rather than solve them – or even grind things to a halt at times!

We'll explore why they can create problems shortly, but first our question is as follows.

Why do people send emails?

For many business settings, and most formal applications, emails do seem to be here to stay. It's because:
- they can be a very apt tool to document important information, sometimes called 'big action,' and information that's long form
- they have the advantage of being asynchronous. That is, they don't take place in real time, which is a plus when dealing with differing global time zones/or domestic shifts for example
- they give people time to gather their thoughts or access information required before they send a reply
- they tend to be written in more guarded, clear, and professional language than instant messaging

So rather than constantly trying to rail against them, we suggest: become more efficient at working out whether they are the best course of action. Sometimes a phone call or walking to a colleague's desk to discuss something can be the best way of dealing with the task in hand!

But if you're sure that email is the way forward, then you need to write them effectively! Because one thing's for sure: who's not overwhelmed by inboxes with hundreds of unread emails? Is it any wonder that people are tempted *to avoid even opening* them? To do so can feel like ploughing the ocean. Time-consuming and over-facing, with the odds of success stacked against them.

And when we're overwhelmed what is likely to happen? There are a few possibilities:

- You freeze and don't do anything, hoping they'll go away! *(They usually don't)*
- You prioritise *(but you may have a nagging doubt about whether you prioritised correctly – unless the sender has been clear)*
- You may ignore, and in time delete them unread *(not ideal)*
- You may feel pressured to perform and bust your bandwidth *(definitely not good)*
- You may make mistakes by replying too quickly and not really answering ALL the points in question *(recipients won't like this, and things might escalate: more work!)*
- You may come over as robotic, and not revealing your uniqueness that a considered reply would show *(and your personal and human uniqueness is your career advantage, the central theme of this book!)*

What do you do to make emails work?

AI tools can really help for certain aspects
Do use these tools for the 'non-human' aspects of communication, such as:
- Inbox management and organisation
- Punctuation and grammar suggestions (though you'll still need to 'be in charge'!)
- Editing suggestions
- Automated follow-up reminders
- Spam and security protection

And there may be other functions you can think of, so do list them now, before we move on next to the functions where the human touch is definitely required for optimal results.

The Subject line is your first superpower!
Once you have established that email is the right medium, make your emails stand out right from the start – with the right subject heading.

The subject has the greatest potential for effective communication. So why does it tend to be the most overlooked? Think about it, how many countless strings have you seen referring to forwarded emails, replies, replies to forwarded emails . . .? Maddening.

Even worse can be vague subjects like *Friday,* or *Update.* Update on what? Does my computer need updating? Are you just casually updating me on what your cat had for breakfast? That's a chat: not an email topic!

As we all try to protect our bandwidth and conquer those hundreds of emails, Subject lines that aren't on point are the ones most likely be overlooked or de-prioritised.

And be careful if you think that your subject line: *Progress update first quarter* is reusable in second quarter, without updating. People do that, and how can that be efficient, impactful writing? No, it's sloppy.

You might think about rewriting the subject every time there's a new reply in. This also keeps an AI summary going of what the next steps/inputs/status of the chain might be. This can work very well except where there is a very clear audit trail involved, where an original title for a key topic needs maintaining. That said, even if you have to stay with a title such as: *'Project Jupiter'* don't still use your update on *'Project Jupiter Q2'* when you're referring to an update on 'Project Jupiter Q3'!

How to design a crystal-clear subject heading

And yes, we use that verb 'design' to highlight what we mean. You need to craft an email for success, right from the start. Be the agent of your success: know in your mind what the purpose of the email is, both for you and for your reader. Effective writing makes impact and gets read.

You could consider something on these lines:
- *Urgent Funding Decision Required Now*
- *Support needed to avoid Critical Project Delay*
- *Your Presentation Inputs needed by Feb 28*

This is one of the simplest things you can do in your everyday working life to help streamline your communications. Give it a try!

Then develop your main themes

'So what?' and Calls to Action are needed more now than ever:
- Not just to get to the point
- But also to engage the overwhelmed or the disinterested
- To connect
- To get results

So we could easily outline our **which4words** here, with explanatory words following in brackets, as:

1. **Get-to-the-point** – (ok, we're cheating a bit using hyphens, but you know what we mean!)
2. **Engage** – (in the sense readers understand: Why me?)
3. **Connect** – (in the sense readers understand and connect to the follow-on question: So what?)
4. **Results** – (Oh good, that's what we're after)

Would you agree? Or what might *your* **which4words** be?

You'll see that we're focusing *on how readers will react* to the emails they receive.

Hold that thought in your head. What expressions would you hope to see?

Think not only about **which4words** but **which4words and a picture**, even if it's only in your mind!

We're all about the human touch throughout this book, and if it can cut through the noise and make impact, so much the better!

So do design emails (and indeed all your business writing), so that you the writer, and your readers all concur, as far as possible in most of your writing tasks, that *'Yes, that's what we're after.'*

How do you write to get your desired results?

1. If you're initiating the message

    All the points in our 4-step writing system in Chapter 6 apply here too. Email may appear informal but the more traditional 'rules of engagement' apply as to your other writing. Here too, focus on writing that conveys a handshake, drawing the person or people you are writing to in, not pushing them away.

    Whereas it's important to get to the point:

    –   Context matters
    –   Civility and agreeableness too

2. If you're replying

    Mirroring style, up to a point at least, can be a helpful thing to promote goodwill. But naturally only do this if the language directed at you is professional and courteous!

    We've pointed out earlier in the book how important opening and closing salutations are. If the person you're replying to has left out 'Hi' or 'Dear' to you or signed off simply 'Regards' we don't suggest you do too. It's less likely to draw the person towards you.

3. Some pitfalls

    Even if you're assiduously using your AI tools to help, some pitfalls remain if you don't have your human antennae out!

    The most common can be:

    - A lack of nuance – people can't see the expression in your face, so your words need to convey that (preferably in a personable way!)
    - Expecting people to reply instantly to your email. It's not the nature of the medium: that's what instant messaging is about
    - Not appreciating that email can so easily be passed on, perhaps unknowingly, to others who weren't the intended recipients

Regarding this last point, we see numerous examples of leaked sensitive information or private data. Interestingly, this might not just be by human error in forwarding the email on, but by the automated email route – as the following case study shows.

CASE STUDY – ANZ Bank Australia

Amongst many other news sites, the BBC reported in August 2025 (BBC News, 2025), that one of Australia's largest banks had apologised to staff who found out they had been fired through an automated email asking them to hand back their laptops.

ANZ's retail banking executive, Bruce Rush, said it was "not our intention to share such sensitive news with you in this way" as the firm cuts jobs in its retail banking business.

The bank said the emails were sent to some staff ahead of schedule, and therefore in error. It said it has since stopped sending the emails and that they had now spoken to staff personally.

The Financial Sector Union were on the case and were less forgiving. They opined that the email caused 'panic and distress' and was a result of the company forcing through a 'chaotic pace of change'.

Sadly, scenarios like this are manifold. When will people learn?

Instant Messaging (IM)

Instant messaging, like text messaging, is the ideal medium for quick fire messages in real time. They are usually, though not exclusively, used to message colleagues within an organisation, or to message people on social media. It can also take the form of live chat in customer service. And that rather describes how IM can so often be taken: as chat. And chat can so often lead nowhere. Hardly ideal when it comes to the effective outcomes needed in business.

If you are going to use it at work, do draw up some rules of engagement. There are plenty out there. And do refer back to Chapter 2 where we talk about what we call *The Five Pings Syndrome* to refresh your memory on how IM can be a great help where instant updates and keeping people in the loop are needed, but a hindrance when it causes distractions and incomplete communication.

When what people call 'big action' or sensitive or legal matters and the like are involved, email is likely to the better option, providing an identifiable audit trail too.

Letters

Letters still feature in today's business writing, usually where a level of formality is required. This might be for matters of legal or financial importance, or sensitive personal information such as health records or HR situations or complaints. They are increasingly sent electronically, although they can still be sent in paper form, via traditional mail.

AI tools can provide the right layouts for the task in hand, which is a great help both for companies and individuals. When it comes to content, so many of our tips so far, especially those in regard to writing emails, can come into play. These will include:
- Planning the letter before you start writing: its purpose, and the outcomes you want, alongside focusing on the receiver's needs
- Making sure you reflect your values and your organisation's values just as you expect to do in all your communication. Consistency matters
- Making sure you address your letter correctly to the right person (checking you have written their name correctly), at the right address, at the right time
- Making sure you have a concise and meaningful subject heading
- Making sure you are clear, professional, and personable in the letter
- Signing off in a professional, respectful, and personable manner
- Checking you have included any additional documentation you allude to
- Checking accuracy before you send
- Checking outcomes/follow-up after you've sent, as necessary
- Assessing: Did the letter work as expected? If not, why not?

Meetings and follow-up (see also Reports)

The number of employees engaged in meetings does of course vary depending on the company and role, but according to research by Fellow (fellow.ai, 2025), the average employee who does need to attend meetings spends 11.3 hours per week in meetings or approximately 28% of the work week. That is the average: in areas such as project work or software development, this will likely be considerably more. Why is this?

Perhaps the other written tools at our disposal are not being used to their full potential. For any manager of teams, this is an alarming statistic.

So although this book is not about whether to hold meetings or not, and AI can help you decide, we can give tips on the human written element in and around them, as follows:

Agendas
- People do need to be informed, usually by email, about the purpose of the meeting and the desired outcomes
- The details of the place and time need to be sent to the right people at the right time

Sounds obvious? Believe us, it doesn't always happen!

Necessary supplementary information can be supplied at this stage too, maybe a pre-read (see the next section)

The curious case of the Pre-Read
Let's look at one digital tool that you may or may not favour.

Businesses had to cope with the sudden onslaught of Zoom Meetings during the pandemic, and this has carried on into a post-pandemic world. For a time it felt like the way to deal with this was to invent, dust-off or at least extoll the virtues of the 'pre-read.'

What's a pre-read you might be asking? Well, it is quite self-explanatory: before any meeting of note, some companies require that a short summary be sent up front of the content of the meeting. This can include key takeaways, decisions required etc. to ensure these valuable video sessions were used in as effective a way as possible.

But many question whether this is truly effective. Isn't it an extra task to be shoehorned into a day, probably already chocked full of zoom meetings and task duplication?

All too often businesses notice that pre-reads were not being pre-read at all! At best they can be something that's simply glanced at during meetings. So that's not actually effective writing is it? As a result companies like Amazon insist upon people reading 'reports' together in real time during management meetings and working through the content together.

The clear objective is to specifically deep dive into complex topics in a mindful manner.

Exercise

It would be good to discuss this topic with others. Have you encountered this subject? What's your view as to what works best in the interest of effective communication?

Meetings notes/Minutes

Meetings notes are, as you would expect, the record what's happened in meetings and the follow up needed. Minutes are the form of meetings notes required in a more formal setting and which can be legally binding.

There are lots of wonderfully helpful AI tools to help with notetaking and collaboration platforms like Microsoft Teams and Slack that that can help share these notes.

That said, we still find people reading these notes incredulously, asking '*Were we at the same meeting?*'

This is because effective writing isn't just about recording what everyone says and writing that up. It can be as much as understanding what's not being said, and what needs to be unearthed, recording that too – and checking people are on the same page. Everyone needs to know, and agree who does what and when, un-equivocally.

Additionally, people who weren't even at the meeting might need to be informed that they have been allocated actions, even if this wasn't actually highlighted in the meeting.

Once again *people* have to be in charge here, to offer the human touch in written follow up that AI isn't able to provide that can be crucial for effective outcomes.

Newsletters

As we're seeing, social media can be a crowded and unpredictable space:
- where comments sections can often erupt into a battle of viewpoints, and
- where the companies running the sites have ever burgeoning algorithms to feed, depending on context and perspective

For this reason, there's a noticeable change happening. Many companies are turning to, rediscovering and simply upweighting their focus on one of the simplest of digital marketing tools: the newsletter.

Research suggests their use in both business to consumer (B2C) and business to business (B2B) settings has increased significantly over the past 3 years (bee-hiiv, 2025).

From a business point of view, having direct access to your contacts (not to mention the legal implications of having their explicit consent) and unfiltered control of the dialogue with them is clearly beneficial.

Another key benefit is the ability to send out long-form information to a captive audience who have signed up to hear from you. Clearly you can't afford to lose their interest by writing waffle so:
- Ensure you write information that's helpful/interesting to them
- Ensure your positive organisation/brand offering shines through

The double focus matters.

Reasons for this resurgence from the consumer perspective

We can summarise the main ones as:

For focus
In an increasingly noisy online world, consumers and clients often feel like zoning in on exactly what it is they are after. That's their first consideration – before they'll then sign up for more regular or detailed information on that specific offering. They find this is a more beneficial use of their time/bandwidth than constantly having to sift through all the other offerings out there.

It's in essence an efficiency drive.

For education
Often people are looking to learn as much as they can about a specific topic – with many savvy business operators offering step-by-step *How-to Guides* to their subscribers.

There are some excellent executions of this out there, where multi-part educational series are explicitly promised, ahead of any sign up.

For curation
There can be a number of reasons why curation can appeal to people:
- perhaps building on their desire to learn

- perhaps focused on wanting personalisation without the hassle of direct communication
- perhaps because as consumers of today, they have access to more variety and offerings than ever before, which makes them more discerning

And of course it can be simply a mix of all of these reasons that explains why consumers are often looking for someone to sift through the various offerings and offer tailored options, personalised to their taste.

For a sense of community

Humans have always felt a need to belong. We are social animals and it's natural for us to seek out others interested in the same things as us, to learn, to share, to experience together. We also (as often mentioned in this book), value the human touch – especially if we are investing our time/money into a product and of course also into a service.

So for many, this social element can be key to the interaction and output they desire.

If an organisation shows its passion for a worthy cause, where they lead others will find it easy to follow when their values align. This is such a powerful use of business writing for good.

As a tool to show pricing/availability

For others, the use of Newsletters can be something they view as purely functional and transactional. They might for example want to be notified when a new batch of an out-of-stock product may come in. Or very often they want to be alerted if there is a sale/price drop/discount code on an item they may have their eye on but haven't quite been able to justify the cost.

Reasons for the resurgence are also from the rise of AI tools

The rise of AI tools to help generate, support, indeed run a Newsletter Programme has definitely played a major role in the elevation of their importance and use.

It's easier than ever before to let a tool help create very specific/hyperpersonalised content, right down to the individual level. This is something that would have required massive effort and therefore cost in the past. It's a huge bonus that newsletters today no longer need to be the generic mass marketing tools they once were – but can be individually tailored to interests, timed milestones or pretty much anything you and your consumer desire.

What might your own potential Newsletter offering be?

Here's an opportunity to think about what your own potential Newsletter offering might be. Use **which4words** to decide what your Newsletter could provide.

Are you looking to cement your role as an expert in a specific field? If so you might choose the following **which4words**:

1. **Knowledge** – (make it clear why you are an expert; how you have gathered this expertise)
2. **Sharing** – (it's your mission to share the joy that comes through knowing your product as you do)
3. **Educate** – (set up a plan for others to generate knowledge, expertise of their own)
4. **Celebration** – (learning should be rewarding, reflect on how to celebrate this)

Alternatively, your focus might simply be on building trust/engagement with consumers through transparent product availability information. Your goal would be to avoid consumers feeling frustrated by the fact they keep missing out on high demand items.

In this scenario, you might choose the following **which4words**:

1. **Transparency** – (what is available, when, at what price)
2. **Context** – (why is the situation the way it is? Could it change?)
3. **Planning** – (what is the best way to secure the product you are after?)
4. **Support** – (reassurance, we will work to get you the product you so desire)

Understanding your approach here clearly and simply can help you tailor all steps in the process: your content, and your call to action (reason to sign up) etc. in order to provide a meaningful and seemingly interactive and personalised experience. Yes, that's the attraction of a *'simple'* yet fully curated newsletter.

Onboarding: a starter checklist for writing effectively

Larger companies will be able to provide well-devised corporate guidelines for business writing tasks (though it's patently clear from some of the examples we've seen in the book so far, that employees don't always follow them!). Start-ups and smaller companies often don't have guidelines in place. So we think it eminently helpful to provide a starter checklist for effective writing for all. They're something to refer back to in all your writing tasks.

The points cover your needs, your organisation's needs, and your stakeholders' needs (and that includes AI as we've mentioned previously). It affects/is affected by your communication – and your clients'/customers' needs.

Be alert and be prepared to ask your bosses and colleagues if you're not sure about any of these. And bosses, we continue to stress this: do realise the importance of offering that support. Everybody needs to pull together: effective communication has to be the gold standard for all.

Go through the list, just as a tick box exercise first, for you to realise the foundations need to be in place as an onboarding procedure so that everyone understands that consistency matters for being true to personal values and for communicating corporate values.

Right from the outset, understand the importance of:

- Correctly writing the names of the people you're addressing. And checking how formally or informally they like to be addressed. Ask them if you're not sure. It matters
- Writing that covers the cultural expectations (including written conventions) of your correspondents. One size won't fit all, and you owe them the courtesy of finding out what they are, as far as you are able. This can cover pronouns too
- Understanding what challenges may be in place for your readers, as well as for yourself, which may include neurodiversity awareness, dyslexia, dyspraxia, Irlen's or other sight issues, and so on. It'll take you time, but your readers deserve this, and don't forget there can be legal requirements to take this into account too
- Realising time zones/public holidays etc. may vary from yours if you are communicating internationally, and so you may be unreasonably expecting early replies to your messages
- Bandwidth – with the meaning here that if your workload is at capacity, flag this up with your stakeholders. Your communication can only be effective if you are on top of it. If you let problems stack up because you stop communicating, they rarely go away as a result of your inaction, which is effectively 'ghosting.' They usually multiply! People get annoyed, things escalate into complaints, results suffer, as does your professional reputation. Flag things up: everyone deserves it!
- Never writing something in the heat of the moment that you would not be prepared to say, let alone slipping into the guise of a 'keyboard warrior' if annoyed. This can so easily, however unintentionally, land you into the tricky realm of defamation. Don't go there!

Personalisation journey for onboarding

- Beyond disseminating writing guidelines, it's important to tell people what's happening in the business and get their involvement
- An integral part of this is to get to know something about them: birthday, life milestone etc. – something that recognises them as an individual

Outsourcing Marketing/Advertising etc? Check and check again to avoid pitfalls!

It's always been important that if you decide to outsource this type of work to others, for example freelancers, agencies and so on, you need to check content for correctness before it gets published, which will be in *your name*. But now, with the rise and ease of use of AI tools, it's a point that's particularly important to reinforce.

Never assume that any content generated by anyone, or anything else is correct. Even if it seems ok at first glance, check, re-check, check again.

One case where this didn't happen came during the holy grail of traditional advertising: the Superbowl 2025. In a bid to highlight the benefits of its AI tool, Gemini, Google aired an ad showing how the tool had helped a local cheesemonger to create a valuable marketing campaign, as reported in The Guardian (Hall, 2025).

A section of the copy created stated that a type of cheese, Gouda, accounts for *'50 to 60 percent of global cheese consumption'* – a statistic that many were quick to point out as incorrect.

Google had to subsequently change the advert, but they'd taken a hit to their reputation. This serves as a great example of how even the biggest companies, with the biggest budgets, and smartest people and tools available, can often fail in the most basic of steps.

Presentations

It's good to ask people whose presentation they have recently enjoyed and why. And if they say "none" then that's an indicator that something needs to be done differently!

One reply we received gives a clear snapshot of a presentation that worked. It was a Chief Finance Officer's presentation, highly rated because of the impact it made.

So, digging deeper how did he achieve it? It was because:
- It was well formatted – easy for the audience to navigate by themselves

- It was well presented – the boss understood that he was paid to 'shoulder the burden' of the detail, and his job as presenter was to distil the message to his (largely non-financial) audience
- He provided context and what had happened to date
- He outlined the opportunity that presented
- He ended with *A Clear Ask*

Although the audience were not necessarily going to fully understand the financial ins and outs, they understood the impact. And impact can engage the disinterested alongside the already interested, and carry *everyone* forward if developed in the right way.

Looking at each slide, the written words on each made sense on their own.

They additionally made even more sense with the embellishment he was able to offer when talking. He could deal with the nuances that his audience might raise. As we have mentioned throughout the book, he was able to answer questions that *his fellow humans might raise, with their ability to read between the lines.*

Reports – 'one size won't fit all'

Have you ever been asked to write a report? Did you struggle to know where to start? Should it be a long, detailed report? A shorter, targeted report? Or perhaps even just a summary?

There's an art in sharing information. You should always consider:
- the purpose of the information sharing moment
- as well as the stakeholder group concerned

to help define the specific format. Whatever your search engine tells you, and yes, there's so much information out there, much of it very helpful, don't be duped into thinking there's a 'one size fits all report.'

Use your human uniqueness to select the right tool for the right moment, the right stakeholder group

Larger companies often have well defined reporting requirements. Indeed many management systems define exact requirements through structures such as Management and Control Reporting Systems (MCRS) or similar. Specific project management methodologies such as AGILE also clearly define the flow of information/tasks at every interval and step.

Looking into such processes and asking AI to help you will provide you clear examples as to what's needed in specific instances. But it's for *you* to consider these questions and examples before you generate a report, in any of its forms.

1 Who are the Stakeholders?

Understanding who is going to be reviewing the information is probably the most important starting point.

Taking the example of a project you may be running:

A status update report issued to your team, charged with the immediate deliverables might:

- focus specifically on shorter term deliverables
- whilst still referencing the overall status for context

A project update to a senior steering committee would most likely require:

- a lower level of detail
- a broader range of subjects – usually being a cross functional affair not only to tackle important issues such as funding, but also prompting decisions, risk mitigation, alignment work etc

A deep dive report for a top management meeting with for example the main client, or your MD/CEO, might be required – to focus on one specific issue. An example could be:

- a financial decision required above a certain threshold
- or a safety incident where every single detail about the event and its future impact on processes might be required

In all cases, you'll need to consider whether:

- it's a formal update to an external stakeholder that requires specific contract details to be researched, referenced and correct?
- or is the report the result of someone requesting more on the analytical or creative side of things?

For the former some milestones/facts and figures might be more appropriate. For the latter, a more qualitative summary of where the project's at.

Your individuality comes in here: reflect on it. AI can't provide you with the reflection you need to take everything into account. No, your brain is required here! You need to reflect on:

- what needs to be covered with regard to the subject concerned
- how to match the needs of your stakeholders

- how to avoid potential but unnecessary additional work
- how to eliminate information overload for those on the receiving end of your
  reports – whilst still providing sufficient context

2 The interval/frequency of the report

Certainly within a corporate environment, the type/interval at which the report appears, can help dictate its content.

An annual report – for example a company's financial statements, or a year in review for a department or a team, typically requires detailed information with a lot of data and deep dives on various topics.

A monthly report would usually also be far reaching, focusing on achievements and issues/risks whilst providing metrics – for example progress towards goals/Key Performance Indicators (KPIs) or Objectives and Key Results (OKRs). It might include a changing monthly deep dive topic where additional visibility may be welcomed.

A weekly report would most likely be more action driven: focusing on action logs (who does what and when and outcomes) or specific areas for focus for a team or individual.

Daily communications would also most likely be at a task level – specific inputs required or tasks to be completed.

3 Format of the report

If there's a requested format for the report, you need to work with that, adjusting your style and checking that others are too.

If a PowerPoint update is requested, and this is to be presented in person, then a storyline built around a few charts/images might be more appropriate. Do check out our specific tips on storytelling in Chapter 6.

If a formal Word Document has been requested, you'll find many templates that can help. But a longer more structured/detailed document is most likely expected.

For daily updates, check whether emails will be the right medium. Keep them short, to the point – perhaps referencing how/where additional information (such as a project SharePoint/Common Drive) might be available if desired.

4 To summarise: don't be afraid to clarify what's needed

So to summarise, what stakeholders are often looking for when asking for a report is:

- either a summary or status update of where things are at
- understanding if there are any delays/concerns/risks – or wanting very specific
  detailed information on a very specific topic

Either way use the tips above and do ask if you're not sure about how to write 'the right report.' You need to protect your own bandwidth alongside keeping your stakeholders happy.

The **which4words** that help us plan here are:

1. **Why?**
2. **Stakeholders**
3. **Format**
4. **Story**

Would these work for you? If not, **which4words** could be your springboard to action and efficiency?

Social media

Social media is one huge area that's a daily part of many of our working lives. This can be either directly if we create content ourselves, or indirectly, each time we 'like', share, support, or discuss content that others have created.

The range is vast. There are an almost unlimited number of platforms, uses and indeed approaches we can take. There's lots of advice out there on how you can do this, but let's for a moment think back to Purpose. What are you actually trying to achieve?

Selecting a platform

The very first thing in this connection is to think about where to post. That's something you'd do before you think about writing your post in the style that suits the platform.

Let's look at a case study in three parts that should help you organise your thoughts.

CASE STUDY – Where to post
PART ONE: Recruitment
A financial manager in a medium sized organisation is looking to hire six new recruits over the coming 12 months.

Following all necessary procedures, they've handed over the formal recruitment to their HR/Personnel team. But the financial manager has the insider knowledge that the market is competitive. They want to do their bit to make their team and these positions seem attractive in advance to potential applicants.

So which platform immediately comes to your mind?

The go-to for postings such as this would typically be a professional networking site such as LinkedIn or XING, to name but two. Sites such as these attract a raft of prospective applicants for the roles advertised. As a result they have developed a multitude of tools and algorithms dedicated to facilitating results. They would hopefully maximise your reach and impact.

Once the platform is clear – understanding the specifics of that platform and of course their users will help to write the copy/content effectively. You have already used **which4words** to define what the job is about and what candidate you are looking for – but if we stick with LinkedIn as an example – successful posts typically:
- Are concise – aim for 150 words or less
- Feature mobile friendly formatting – think short sections using bulleting e.g.
    - What the role demands
    - Development and delivery of multichannel marketing campaigns
    - Internal and External Stakeholder Management etc.
- Include Calls to action e.g. *Are you excited to join a dynamic, growing marketing team?*
- Cover all major points candidates would expect to see including salary range, location, experience level, job content, profile expectations

And as for the don'ts, simply reverse this list. Lengthy, text-heavy posts that are vague and require decoding and deciphering are a no-no.

PART TWO: Rebranding

Here's a quite different scenario. A marketing manager has been tasked with totally rebranding a cosmetics brand that has been around for the last 50 years but has seen a dramatic downturn in sales. The company wants:
a) to modernise the brand and introduce its hard-earned reputation for quality to a new, younger demographic
b) the rebranding exercise to offer a focus, in parallel, on interaction and securing as much feedback as possible during the process

Now what would you recommend? Still LinkedIn? It may be used to unveil the final output as more of a professional update but platforms such as Instagram or TikTok might offer more relevant and targeted access to the demographic – whilst offering multiple streams/feeds to maximise interaction at the same time.

Examples of the types of content and language you could use could be as follows:

- Building excitement – for example by use of *'sneak peeks,' 'first looks'* or even product *'teasers'* can help to create buzz about a change that may be coming
- Encourage participation – again calls to action, encouraging user generated content or sharing, challenges, competitions, sharing through specific hashtags. Any language that encourages active participation can dramatically help consumers identify with and therefore like a brand
- Solicit direct feedback – use polls, questions, interact with comments. Include the consumer in the process and likely they will connect at a deeper level

But as we can't stress enough, be mindful of the need for *consistency.*

Talk about why you are making the change, whilst maintaining key messaging and core brand attributes from the previous branding, to make sure your Ask Engine Optimisation (AEO) footprint hasn't been negatively affected (see *Websites* later in the chapter).

PART THREE: A sales activation
And here's yet another example. A local beer brewer would like to celebrate its 100-year anniversary by giving away free beer to their loyal customers, at their main outlet in the city where they are based.

So ask yourself the question: where would you head to first from a social media point of view? Platforms such as Facebook, and more specifically local city or regional groups within that platform, might be an excellent way of reaching the specific intended audience. On the other hand, if your goal is just about gaining *as much reach as possible* for a specific announcement, you might find a multi-platform coordinated approach is your best way forward. Then you might think of attention-grabbing writing, such as:

"🎉 FREE BEER GIVEAWAY! 🎉"

Giving away free beer is a very exciting pull for many people. So yes it's worth shouting about it to the target market, as something they shouldn't miss out on.

So we have the bold attention-grabbing headline, but further details also need to be seen at a glance, making it very clear what happens next.

This could be through the use of bulleting to make it as simple as possible for users to understand, but also, very importantly, *to share:*
- *When? Saturday 1st December – 14.00.-16.00*
- *Location – Dave's Drinks – 23 Spring Street*
- *Limited – 1 Case of free beer per Family (while stocks last)*

Then you could include further wording, such as:

"Spread the message, share the joy, support local business!"

And you could develop the post further, about loyalty and gratitude:

"We're proud to support local business and the community and are delighted to take the opportunity to show our appreciation of our valued customers with this spectacular offer. Be sure to be there!".

Whatever the case, understand what *'good should look like'* and write accordingly.

Being mindful of tone/Do's and Don'ts

By now you'll have a growing awareness of the tone expected at each of the social media platforms. You'll be identifying the words that users expect to see and what they don't. Naturally, many of you might be finding it second nature knowing how to approach each platform for maximum impact. But in all cases it never hurts to recap some of the basics.

Principal social media platforms currently used in business

Facebook

Overall Facebook tends to be informal, even casual, unlike platforms like LinkedIn which is markedly more professional in tone.

Facebook and similar platform users focus on posting and expecting community content. We could say their focus is on building or belonging to the community/communities in question.

So how would you write? It could work best to tailor your posts to focus on community first and personal second. Me, me, me tends to be met with resistance.

Using images, stories and descriptive language can help to bring a personal touch to business stories – this is after all a platform about people, human connection, about community.

So imagine you have written a book – a real passion project of yours! And you'd like to drum up support for it with your network. Let's first think of **which4words** might be relevant for your goals:

🚀 *Hey digital marketing friends!*

Big news – I'm launching a new book all about mastering digital marketing in an AI-driven world.

This book dives into how AI is reshaping strategies, tools, and audience engagement —and what every marketer needs to know to stay ahead.

If you're curious about blending creativity with AI tech for better results, this one's for you! Would love your support:

✏ Check it out when it drops
💬 Share your thoughts or questions here
🔁 Pass this along to anyone in marketing who's ready for the future

Let's talk AI + marketing and make sure we're leading the pack!

#DigitalMarketing #AIinMarketing #MarketingStrategy #FutureOfMarketing #MarketingCommunity #BookLaunch #MarketingTips

Once again, it's essential to maintain consistency across the various posts to ensure common themes – but tailor/tweak according to the specific channel.

Instagram

This provides a truly multimedia experience. Instagram, often just referred to as *Insta*, started as a way to share images but has developed so that users now have the ability to share images, sound, video, text – either individually or all combined.

Understanding how to link the various media offered in a single platform, then coordinate them to re-use, amplify and indeed turbo-charge communication can be one of the most powerful professional tools out there. So do your homework and let **which4words** help with a laser beam focus on what you are actually trying to say.

There is an enormous potential for reward if done correctly, but also a huge potential to confuse and alienate if done incorrectly.

Very interestingly, as we write, Instagram is suggesting a reduction in the number of hashtags people use, from 30 to just 3! It highlights exactly what we're saying throughout: getting to the point matters!

LinkedIn

What tone would you expect on a professional platform such as LinkedIn? Most users are there for purely professional business purposes, so keeping language professional, short, to the point tends to be the norm.

Professionals using the site often check the site briefly during breaks or after work hours. So if you structure your text in a way that people can quickly scan and understand at a glance, it's sure to reap benefits, both for you and for them.

The use of clear headings, bullet points for key takeaways and, you guessed it, **which4words**, can help connect with the busy users of the platform.

Try and focus on 'what's in it for the reader' using hashtags to summarize/highlight key themes. This will in turn help people looking for such information – but who might not be direct connections – still manage to find your posts.

So let's stick with the preceding example in Facebook about your imaginary book launch, but make the language a little more formal and targeted to the professional group you're part of:

1. **Announce**. This is the first time you are sharing this big news with the world! It should act as a big reveal.
2. **Summarise.** You've never spoken about this before: now is your chance to distil the essence of what the book is about into a short, succinct summary.
3. **Support.** You're looking to your network to help spread the news, but hopefully also buy your book! You are grateful to your network for their support.
4. **Maximise.** You want maximum reach/exposure and therefore want to tailor your post to make sure the platform's algorithm supports you spreading your message as far as possible.

So with all that in mind, how about the following:

Big news – my new book is officially on its way!

After months of writing, refining, and rewriting, I'm thrilled to share insights on the future of digital marketing in an AI world. As most of us are not ready for the changes ahead, what can we do about it now, not only to prepare, but to thrive in this exciting new world?

This project has been both the biggest challenge but also privilege of my professional career to date, and I'm excited to finally show it to the world.

Here's how you can help bring this book to life:

Follow the page for launch updates

Leave a comment or share your thoughts on the topic

Share this post to help spread the word

Your support means everything — thank you for being part of this journey.

#NewBook #BookLaunch #ThoughtLeadership #BusinessBooks #AuthorJourney #Publishing #Leadership #Entrepreneurship

TikTok

This is a much more demographic and style-specific platform than many others. Users here tend to know exactly what 'hook' will pull them in and what won't. You'll need to do some dedicated homework – for example TikTok's own Content Creator advice or third parties, such as successful online marketing expert Gary Vaynerchuck (@garyvee), can be a great starting point.

Short form and video as main media may be at the forefront of the platform's approach, but super clear attention grabbing and self-explanatory text (with attention grabbing design to match) must capture attention and imagination *within the first seconds of appearing.*

Anchor into platform trends whilst steering towards your own business goals with concrete actions or next steps for users at the end of the content (should you have managed to keep their attention until then!).

For example, as we write, there's a viral trend on TikTok where users try and position their mouths to make it look as if they have only one tooth. This could be a great moment for a company specialising in dental hygiene to get involved!

Or the *"She's always MIA"* trend – where users, inspired by the lyrics of a certain song (in this case *Mrs Hollywood* by Go-Jo), post 2 pictures of themselves in a carousel format. The first picture is typically polished and glamorous, the second highlighting their real self, quirky unpolished or even nerdy image of themselves. This could present an ideal opportunity for a number of brands to identify with and/or support users to be their comfortable everyday self.

X (previously known as Twitter)

A key contender to be considered as the originator of the short form social media post, being concise is key on X. That said, the original limitation of just 140 characters per post has been increased to 280 characters per post, because being too concise can mean that key messages are over simplified!

Bullets, lists, **which4words** – these will all help to get to the point. You must stand out as far as possible in thousands of other posts!

Cross-referencing, linking, tagging, or associating yourself with existing posts, users, or trending topics through clever use of # and @s can allow you to say much more in a very small number of characters.

Be mindful of the fact that there can often be a political undertone to such platforms, whether explicit or implicit. Do refer back to our point on how you need to reflect on your intended purpose before you write any messages at all.

Always keep in mind what you want your business to be known for if that's the identity you portray on the platform. Keep that identity and professionalism to the fore. And even if you are posting as a private individual, remember people can work out your professional links too. Be consistent, don't stray into unguarded comments which may be at odds with your personal and professional values. Reputations matter, in the round.

YouTube. Videos . . . but with an increasing focus on script writing

We round out this section with either the most or least obvious platform depending on your point of view: YouTube!

Although readily known for its video content, YouTube has actually become one of the most important platforms for good business writing skills. Why, you might ask.

Well let's start with the straightforward skill it requires: to create short, attention-grabbing titles, thumbnails or feeding the clickbait dynamic. Examples are punchy tag lines that create intrigue: for example *'We can't go on'* which lead the user into believing the channel might end, when what really happened is the battery ran out on the creator's video camera! This approach is something that the algorithm seems to favour.

But increasingly, YouTube is a platform full of *professionally* created and curated video content. It's now often created by, or at least supported by, large legacy media companies/creators as they all increasingly realise the huge reach and potential revenue streams YouTube offers.

Even 'regular' content creators now approach content creation with a more defined approach to structure, employing editors, videographers and even signing major brand sponsorship deals. The platform has become big business.

So how does professional writing fit in? The answer is simple – script writing. In order for a video to be as good as it can be, as simple to understand as possible:
- We find creators often now script their content well in advance
- This script increasingly becomes the central focus – with the rest of the visuals created around it, often by other contributors such as graphic designers

Also with the rise of AI, a lot of videos are now generated, even narrated, by bots, again around a central script created by the actual channel owner/content creator.

So we find a rather surprising phenomenon that, more than ever before, business writing is the key input across multiple media.

That's why a structured approach, using **which4words,** will help you figure out what you want to say, how you want to say it and make all of your content the best it can be.

When social media is used for direct sales, accurate descriptions matter

Social media has changed in the role it plays for many businesses, and this applies to the role it can play in direct sales. Whereas in the past, social media was largely viewed as being about PR, Marketing Communications, or dialogue with consumers, today many social media platforms are direct sales channels in their own right. They offer the ability to buy and/or sell directly, or indirectly.

Even if a consumer is not purchasing products directly through social media, the interlinked nature of e-commerce today means it's often the landing point or starting point for many a consumer/supplier relationship.

As such, do be mindful that, more than ever, the descriptions of any items or products, even services you may offer, must be as accurate as possible.

There are countless examples of items arriving being completely at odds to what is expected. For example, it could be a lamp shade that arrived in a totally different colour to that shown on the social media post.

If we take the example of samplers and trial packs, posts often feature mountains of product – to illustrate the variety such packs might offer. But when consumers receive the small samples that actually arrive in the mail, they're left disappointed at the tiny amount of product received in reality. That's a poor business outcome.

CASE STUDY – There are consequences when a description is totally misleading
The most extreme examples even go into the fundamental nature of the product itself . . .

A virtual assistant on social media recently targeted a colleague. The product touted was a little robot with a speaker and camera, which can drive around talking, interacting, and seemingly passing on messages to other people.

He thought it might be a light-hearted motivational tool in an office environment. Fortunately, he did some further research before purchasing and discovered it was actually built as a totally different product. It was essentially a doorbell camera with wheels: a security product meant to remotely monitor vacant properties for peace of mind when away. Talk about misleading . . .

So make sure your descriptions are accurate. Use simple hacks like writing clearly:
- what colours are available, for example, and that the purchaser must specify which they want
- or that the delivered product might/will be different in appearance if that's the case

Effective writing avoids misleading customers. Ineffective writing will likely lead to a raft of 1-star reviews, damage to your brand, and likely a lot of additional work in customer service!

That said, we do have to add a rather surprising observation in our next subheading!

When Viral Marketing can be intentionally incorrect!

Indeed, as we mentioned in Chapter 2 we saw how typos in letters and documentation can cost on a financial level and how people can be annoyed if their personal details are wrong, as another example.

But have you ever wondered if people notice typos, generally speaking? Do people care if something is misspelled? Surely an incorrect letter here and there won't have a big impact . . .

Well, there's an interesting viral marketing trend that actually tests this theory and, dare we say it, even has a little fun with it.

Let's take the example of a successful 2025 marketing campaign for the beer brand Coors Light. In large billboards and various other large-scale activations, the company put out a lot of content with large imagery and simple bold text saying:

'Coors Light – Mountain Cold Refershment' (Molson Coors Beverage Company, 2025)

Did you spot the mistake? Well thousands of people did, and they were either delighted or appalled at the fact that such a big company could spell *refreshment* incorrectly as *refershment.* After a lot of interaction both from users through social platforms, as well as enquiries from traditional media, the company issued a statement acknowledging the mistake as the consequence of the being written on Monday – because let's face it – no-one is concentrating on a miserable Monday anyway . . .

It later transpired that yes, it was intentional from the start and led into a whole series of activities including temporarily rebranding to *'Monday Light.'* It serves as a great example of how people do notice and react to inaccuracy.

Another somewhat simpler example was the rebranding of the sportwear company *'Puma'* to *'Pvma'* (News18, 2025). This kick-started much online discussion. Was there a meaning behind this? Was it a mistake, or something else?

So we can see that, from a marketing perspective, if things are written intentionally wrongly, and brands actively position this in order to get noticed and to garner discussion and interaction, then, in the words of Oscar Wilde: *"The only thing worse than being talked about, is not being talked about".*

So get it right or at least get it wrong for a reason!

Notification Culture

"Leave a like, comment, subscribe and hit the bell icon so you never miss another post again!"

Recognise this in social media? Then you're probably fully aware that algorithms are often built to reward consumer engagement with a focus on Notifications and the regular interaction that can ensue.

If people connect with your content and your brand, the social media platforms encourage them to enable notifications, so they can keep up with your posts. And many of us set up feeds, summaries – indeed a culture of notifications – to help us distil and remind us of the core content we are interested in. This can all save time in our busy lives.

But what does that mean for us all as business writers? As content creators? How should we adapt accordingly?

Typically, feeds or daily summaries will focus on two main things only:
1. The title of the post/thread/subject
2. The author

So always keep this in the back of your mind.

Let's look at this case study.

CASE STUDY – Producers of natural essential oils

Producers of natural essential oils are active on a community group dedicated to oils and their consumers on Facebook.

They have a good following and are aware they have their best results when they offer occasional discounts to their loyal followers. These are dedicated followers who have requested notifications on the group.

Which of the following post titles do you think might catch the most attention?

New Post -Tuesday Update – New Launches and Offers

Or

New Post – FLASH SALE! 30% Off

Yes, the second. This may seem obvious, but all too often the key information is buried in text or sub-text and *not visible immediately* in summary or notification form. An easy fix!

Be mindful also of specific timed actions: that is, cadence and frequency. If notifications are an important way of interacting with your audience, you don't want to overload them. Plan what you want to say and use the natural impact the tool brings. If you set off a notification multiple times a day, are people likely to still pay attention, or will you be drowned out with the rest of the noise?

Task boards/To-do lists

In the past many people kept informal to-do lists for themselves, to keep track of important or time-sensitive actions that they did not want to overlook. When working physically in groups or teams, people often used a whiteboard. This was to capture thoughts and be something that other team members could refer back to.

Now, there's a major shift in the business writing landscape with the advent of digital tools such as Asana, Jira etc. These have now become living documents often accessed by multiple people from multiple locations.

Not only does this mean:
- you need to focus more on their creation – with the understanding that a working document for others will likely need more detail/context than perhaps your own shorthand reminders for yourself might have done
- it will also require a concerted coordination or administration effort to review changes, ensure progress meets the output desired, and clarify questions that will arise as others work together

The shift can be incredibly powerful if well managed, but potentially disastrous if you try to translate it 1–1 from a rough personal reminder.

Websites and search optimisation generally

Writing for websites is of course a specialist subject not within the remit of this book. But it is helpful to point out here how:
- your tone of voice directly influences online presence in a modern digital world and
- how consistency matters

This might be a surprise to you as it's yet another aspect to the shift in our digital world arising from emerging AI.

Search Engine Optimisation (SEO) v Answer Engine Optimisation (AEO)

You'll know the term Search Engine Optimisation (SEO) in relation to digital marketing. For the past 20 years, this way of building your digital content, websites, even your social media posts, was structured around a focus on backlinking and keyword optimisation that would elevate your content versus the algorithms of the major search engines. This all gave you greater visibility and reach. But now with the rise of AI tools, this is changing.

Answer Engine Optimisation (AEO) is emerging. To cut a long story short, the new AI systems work differently to traditional search engines: aiming to provide direct answers to queries (not links to answers) by scouring the web and looking essentially for two main things:
1. Short, concise, clearly structured, and understandable data
2. Consistency and authority

Tone of voice, consistency and authority matter

So getting to the point, for example using our **which4words** system, can now have a tangible impact on your digital marketing. And just as important (in fact possibly more so) is to reinforce consistency throughout.

Why is that? Well it's because the way AI systems now more holistically evaluate and therefore prioritise/rank content is largely based on consistency.

The more the systems can recognise a clear, unique tone that provides consistent messaging on a topic, the more so called *trust* the systems perceive. And this translates into *authority* on a topic, making it more likely to be shared *as an output to a query*.

In other words, your unique voice, coupled with an ability to communicate clearly and concisely might just be the key to the next chapter of your business presence.

How refreshing not to have to look to others, but inwards to oneself to make strides towards growth!

On this basis, which words would summarise the 'I got-it-moment' for you in this chapter? For us, a **which4word** summary could be:

1. **Optimal** – (use the right approach for the right setting/task)
2. **Informed** – (study the application, setting or platforming question; observe stylistic cues)
3. **Adapt** – (even if it's uncomfortable, adapt your writing based on the setting/ task/platform; cater for your audience instead of trying to persuade them to be more like you)
4. **Consistent** – (no matter the approach, maintain core tone/brand/Compass to ensure consistency across setting/task/platform)

What would your Word Bank to summarise this chapter be?

For this chapter we could suggest a Word Bank as follows:

WORD BANK

Foundation Fundamentals Intrigue Dialogue Active Interactive
Feedback Personal Identity Streamline Smart Sensible Appropriate
Self-Explanatory Goal-Oriented Helpful Inclusive Educational
Tailored Consistent Identity Authority Experience Adapt Optimal

---

What might your Word Bank for this chapter be?

9 Keep the curiosity going: The 'Sherlock Holmes' mindset

This light-hearted chapter is about drawing together everything you've learned so far. It's designed to help you realise how business writing need never be a boring subject!

By now:
- You have worked out how business writing needs to be
  1. Right
  2. Clear
  3. Impactful
  4. Reader-focused
- And as we draw to the conclusion of the book, we hope this has unlocked your inquisitive nature, as this is the best way to continue your learning journey.
- So why not think like Sherlock Holmes and unearth for yourself further secrets of success, by simply looking with fresh eyes at business writing in the world around you – and seeing which work and why?

We're not talking here about 'True Crime' – no, business writing won't ever fall into this genre of writing! But we do want you to have fun being a sleuth one way or another, because even the smallest detail can make a difference as to whether writing works or fails. You just have to look out for them.

The well-known author, Sir Arthur Conan Doyle, brought to us his famous fictional sleuth or 'consulting detective', Sherlock Holmes. Still known globally for 'his powers of observation, deduction and logical reasoning', Holmes drew meaningful conclusions from what could seem the slightest of clues.

We could usefully assume his mantle in this chapter and look at business writing under 'a virtual magnifying glass' to find the clues as to why it works, or why it doesn't. On a more informal basis, we can also glean results by being flâneurs or flâneuses, to use another literary allusion (we told you how reading broadens communication horizons!). We're using these words to describe how sometimes you don't even need that magnifying glass to see what's what. You can just as easily *casually* notice what works and what doesn't in the workplace or the world that you navigate each day!

So, in the spirit of curiosity and unearthing facts about successful communication, look with fresh focus on peoples' linguistic fingerprints.

© 2026 Walter de Gruyter GmbH, Berlin | https://doi.org/10.1515/9783112217696-010

Ask:
- What *should* we be seeing under the gaze of our imaginary magnifying glass, or our casual glance?
- And what *do* we see?

We'll address this in three parts:
1. Be curious about how others see your communication
2. Be curious about how others see your organisation's communication
3. Be curious about the communication you see in the world around you

Part 1: Be curious about how others see your communication

Before we look in more detail at how others communicate, don't forget they'll be making judgments on you too! We've alluded to this earlier and as we approach the end of the book it's good to reinforce the message here.

This time we want you to think about people's *emotional* response, not just whether writing gets the operational results needed. To create great working environments, emotional equilibrium plays a key role in wellbeing.

Visualising people's reactions is a such an easy and useful technique

Remember how we encouraged you in the last chapter:

So let's reinforce this apt message, for effective business writing today!
Think not only about **which4words** but **which4words and a picture**!

Just this tweak gives a different slant to the way we dealt with business writing tasks earlier in the book. And it really suits the way upcoming generations are viewing business writing. Think not just in words but paint a picture in your mind on how people may be reacting to your written messages in a variety of ways, such as:
1. *Yes, can see why this is important – to me/the organisation I work for. Must prioritise*
2. *Can't see why this is a priority right now. It's bottom of my in-tray stuff, and it'll probably get deleted as I've too much else to do*
3. *This is AI generated – what an insult, considering the subject matter (maybe a sensitive matter/a complaint etc.) – I deserve better!*

4. *This isn't professional. Look at the mistakes. It's slapdash too – badly set out/random points. Is this representative of how the writer operates, and their organisation too? And am I not worthy of a professional approach from them?*
5. *I don't trust this message, so it's not going to persuade me. I can't see any professional credibility*
6. *What is this about? I haven't the time or inclination to decode it*
7. *This is terse and borderline rude*
8. *I like the look and feel of this. It's made impact. I'm going to read it*
9. *It's got to the point. And it's friendly. Refreshing and time saving. A result!*
10. *I've got the information I need to make an informed decision. Phew!*
11. *Well thought out: sent to the right people at the right time. We all know what to do and when. Thank you!*

These are all standard reactions. And you might like to add an emoji that works for you, alongside each reaction. It could be an easy reference point because what do you want to see as a result of your written messages? A puzzled face? An exasperated face? A downright cross face? A blank face, not reacting in any way? A pleased face because your writing has worked not just for you but for that person too? Or an expression that shows that the writing was right for the occasion. Of course there are situations where you can't hope for a smiley reaction – equilibrium can be the best you will achieve, but it will show how attuned you are to the situation at hand.

This focus can help develop emotional intelligence too – such an important characteristic if we want to understand, connect, truly resonate with, and build trust with our readers. So let's aim to help people with clear reader-focused messages where we can.

Exercise

Look at these reactions numbered 1–11 again, thinking of yourself as the receiver.

How many written communications have you received in the last week that fit any of these questions? Is a pattern emerging of what people get right and where they get it wrong?

Had you actively considered this before, aspect by aspect?

Now here's an interesting finding. Looking at the reactions, add up the positive ones and then the negatives. Which predominated?

And to our minds there is a clear **which4words** takeaway here:
1. **Clarity** – (why is this message important to me/the organisation?)
2. **Professional** – (trustworthy/mistake-free)
3. **Courtesy** – (there are scenarios when only messages written by humans will do: our readers can deserve that, and they'll appreciate that)

4.   **Results** – (I/we know what to do and why)

What might your **which4words** prompts be here? Which most strike a chord with you? It will help your business writing in the future. Share findings with colleagues too. See how their opinions tally with yours.

Part 2: Be curious about how others see your organisation's communication

We stayed at a hotel recently. Stunning building, scenic location, lovely rooms. But we won't be going back. Why? Sloppy service, dishevelled décor, scruffily turned-out staff with nonchalant attitudes.

We've touched on how this sort of perception can apply to an organisation's written communication too.

So stay curious. Think about how *your organisation* comes over through their communication specifically, and the way they come over in other aspects of their business. There's usually a correlation.

If you were a 'Sherlock Holmes type' sleuth, what's 'the personality of your organisation' you'd see?

Dedicated marketing professionals will have an easy fix on this. But as we're proposing, we all need to have something of the marketer about us as today's workplace writers.

You may not have thought in this way before, so here are pointers to help.

Defining your company's personality: which4words
–   Imagine your company had to write its own CV/resumé now
–   What attributes would appear?
–   How would you convey your company's personality in words?
–   What words can you commit to?
–   What words can your colleagues commit to?

Without a doubt, each of you is intrinsic to the success of the whole. So what are you waiting for? Lose the moment, lose the solution!

Here are some words (in no particular order), that might kick start your exercise:

Market knowledge   Up to date   Innovative   Green
Customer-service-driven   Trustworthy   Dedicated
Value-led   Professional   Reliable   Responsive   Expert
Excelling in latest technology   Responsive   Professional   Friendly
Committed to going the extra mile   Caring

What words would you add?

Use the energy this idea creates and harness it right now to draw up your **which4-words** prompts in this context. Note them down.

Part 3: Be curious. How do you react to writing in the world around you?

This part aims to develop both your analytical and creative writing skills – and shows how you can have fun in the process!

The eyes are off you as you look at the world around you, not necessarily in your work environment, but as part and parcel of your life experience. For example, so many written messages feature in our daily lives as consumers.

Even on hypervisual channels like TikTok, captions matter. In fact TikTok goes as far as giving tutorials on how to write them, acknowledging they're a valuable part of the storyline. Check them out.

Tune in to words and situations: bring out the (latent?) marketer in you!

Once you start to tune in to words, you'll see how important they are in directing readers' attention to the points that advertisers want. In fact let's bring out the (latent?) marketer in you, and you won't ever put it away again!

Want a sofa, for example? Where might you expect the emphasis to be? Comfort? Price? Design? An experience? Look around and you'll see different brands often focusing on just one or two of these factors, for example:

1. *Our top-seller three-seater sofa – Just £799 – yes, you heard that right! Grab this never to be repeated offer, this weekend only!*

2. *Italian artisanry at its best. Deluxe in style, comfort, and elegance. Our range of sofas are a class apart*
3. *Relax in our of-the-moment velvet sofa for two, and let the cares of the day wash away*
4. *Sink down into our squishiest-ever five-person settee and catch up on that valuable family-time in heavenly comfort!*

Can the marketer in you see how the approaches 1 and 2 differ from those in 3 and 4?

We suggest that 1 and 2 are traditional sales pitches, based on knowledge of purchasers' budgets. Examples 3 and 4 have a different pitch: that of both sensory and emotional experience – which is something where a more creative approach comes into play.

Let's look randomly at another sector: airline travel. What might you expect the overriding message to be? Safety? Competitive pricing? Comfort? Customer service? Inclusivity? Again, different airlines will major on different factors.

So we're likely to see advertising messages like these:

We'll find the best prices for you. Click here for huge discounts on your flights/weekend deals on a budget today!

Why do tens of millions of passengers choose to fly with us each year? It's because you'll feel safe and you'll feel welcome. Reliability, with no hidden charges.

Like luxury? Expect superior service? A flight with us treats you as the discerning individual you are, ticks all the boxes and then some!

We won't need to point out the nuances in approach: you'll be seeing them for yourselves.

And really that can be one of the key components of effective business writing. It's not just for the dedicated marketers: it's for us all if we are to capture our uniqueness, our readers' uniqueness, and our common characteristic as humans!

Now over to you! Look at any writing in the world out there

And because we want everyone to realise that business writing involves emotional response (more than many seem to realise), we'd like you to think about *your expression* when you look randomly at the written messages that bombard our senses every day.

So, now become that sleuth, and ask yourself how you feel about each piece of writing you're going to select to take a good hard look at.

Just look at the unsolicited promotional material that land on your doorstep; the adverts that appear everywhere you look. Actively look at each and actively focus on *your* expression! Such as:

Smiling   Quizzical   Confused   Frowning   Expressionless   I-get-it!   Duh!   Great! Thanks   You-got-it!   Fed up   Caught out   Whatever   Results! Incredulous   That's patronising   Stereotypical   Divisive   Fair   Unfair   Credible   Trust-worthy

You could even draw pictures to illustrate – a technique that's particularly helpful for people with dyslexia and that can help us all.

By this method, you'll be putting into practice all the tips and tricks we've shared throughout the book, and we hope you'll be having some fun into the bargain. Become an influencer yourself, sharing the experience with friends and colleagues!

Together you'll be sharpening your powers of observation and processing. You'll tune in to words more effectively. You'll even notice the small print which can be such an eye opener. Suddenly you're not just enticed to buy the latest super-duper product advertised in full-colour close-up splendour, whatever it is, if you see buried in the small print at the bottom: *65% of customers agree* or *80% of our sample of 24 people agreed.* Assess those stats and make an informed decision, which is what humans should be wanting to do!

Words matter. And reading what's there matters.

So use the power you have to choose the right ones to write for your chosen task. Capitalise on it.

Exercise
You can have a lot of fun running microlearning sessions with colleagues on these lines!

What would your Word Bank to summarise this chapter be?

For this chapter we could suggest a Word Bank as follows:

WORD BANK
Curiosity   Exploration   Interrogate   Growth   Development   Looking-glass
Reflection   Passion   Analyse   Observe   Muse   Listen   Process   Evaluate
React   Adapt   Experiment   Reflect   Repeat   Senses   Clues   Influence   Fun
Expressions   Visuals   Feelings   Multi-sensory   Diverse   Capture   Energy

---

What might your Word Bank for this chapter be?

10 The journey continues

We're at the end of the book but your journey continues! We've joined forces with you to realise the impact of:
- The sea-change in the business communication landscape today, largely driven not just by the attention economy but by the emergence of AI tools that are helpful on very many but not all levels, and how we all need to find a way to navigate this new world
- This societal and business disruption that's a leveller for all. Whatever our skills and learning styles and communication approaches, it entails developing flexible and wide-ranging skills, as never before
- Our uniqueness as individuals, with personalities of our own, and the ability to nurture positive communication skills through our life experience, which we should be proud to present to the world
- Our uniqueness as humans, able to benefit from all the digital/AI tools available, whilst also understanding how writing for humans is going to be a key contribution to sustainable business communication success
- Critical thinking skills:
    - understand purpose/your brief
    - frame and ask the right questions to get clarification
    - verify/check credibility (being prepared to challenge if necessary)
    - provide context
    - check quality
    - and ultimately, get your writing right on all the levels required for the task at hand!

We've introduced our ground-breaking way of cutting through the noise, rediscovering the human touch in the digital age – the **which4words** method:
1. As a tool to help you plan every writing task
2. As a tool to help you focus on writing for humans
3. As a useful tool for calibration/summarising
4. As the key to unlocking your uniqueness as an individual, and as a human

and you have had a great deal of practice using it for yourselves throughout the book.

By now, you'll be identifying new patterns and new prompts, all with a central structured approach, so that your communication as a whole should easily fall into place, to produce seamless, meaningful professional business writing in the round.

You will also have started to build your own personal 'Word Banks' which will evolve with you and will give you a rapid start to help you focus quickly.

We've majored on how a picture, even in your mind's eye, can be a very useful adjunct to the **which4words** method to reinforce your communication success.

So we'd like to use a helpful analogy here. Picture a kaleidoscope in your mind if you can. See the beautiful, coloured components that we could say represent the elements of your life experience that we've referred to in the book, coupled with the perspectives you need to cover in each of your business writing tasks.

With your new **which4words** toolkit you can control how these components glide into focus and readily fall into place for the results you need each time.

Now it's over to you:

- to enjoy adding to your learning using the method, and developing this framework throughout your career, which will actually help with every aspect of your communication, personal as well as workplace, spoken as well as written
- *to understand that yes, writing for humans* can really benefit from AI assistance to hit operational targets, but that you need to be at the helm for all the extra reasons we've set out, such as strategy, creativity and trust

What a differentiator to capitalise on! Good luck on your continuing journey!

References

Altman, S. (2025) 'Saying "please" and "thank you" to ChatGPT costs millions: Altman', *USA Today*, 22 April. Available at: https://www.usatoday.com/story/tech/2025/04/22/please-thank-you-chatgpt-openai-energy-costs/83207447007/ (Accessed: 11 December 2025)

BBC Bitesize (2024) 'Using standard and non-standard English', BBC Bitesize, 24 March. Available at: https://www.bbc.co.uk/bitesize/articles/zp9jkty (Accessed: 11 December 2025)

BBC News (2025) 'Bank apologises for firing staff with accidental email', *BBC News*, 29 August. Available at: https://www.bbc.com/news/articles/c776plg6n8vo (Accessed: 12 December 2025)

beehiiv (2025) '2025 state of email newsletters by beehiiv', *beehiiv Blog*, 28 January. Available at: https://www.beehiiv.com/blog/2025-state-of-email-newsletters-by-beehiiv (Accessed: 12 December 2025)

Blankboard Studio (2025) 'Starbucks marketing strategy (2025) – what every brand can learn', *Blankboard Studio Blog*, 22 April. Available at: https://www.blankboard.studio/originals/blog/starbucks-marketing-strategy (Accessed: 12 December 2025)

Braineet (2024) 'My Starbucks Idea: An open innovation case study', *Braineet Blog*, 4 April. Available at: https://www.braineet.com/blog/my-starbucks-idea-case-study (Accessed: 12 December 2025)

British Dyslexia Association (2025) *Dyslexia*. Available at: https://www.bdadyslexia.org.uk/dyslexia (Accessed: 10 December 2025)

Coates, S. (2025) 'Can we trust ChatGPT despite it "hallucinating" answers?', *Sky News*, 9 June. Available at: https://news.sky.com/story/can-we-trust-chatgpt-despite-it-hallucinating-answers-13380975 (Accessed: 11 December 2025)

Coldwell, W. (2024) '"I received a first but it felt tainted and undeserved": inside the university AI cheating crisis', *The Guardian*, 15 December. Available at: https://www.theguardian.com/technology/2024/dec/15/i-received-a-first-but-it-felt-tainted-and-undeserved-inside-the-university-ai-cheating-crisis (Accessed: 10 December 2025)

Clyde and Co (2025) *Lessons from Hamburg Commissioner for Data Protection on AI and credit decision-making*. Available at: https://www.clydeco.com/en/insights/2025/10/lessons-from-hamburg-commissioner-for-data-protect (Accessed: 11 December 2025)

Cybernews (2025) *ChatGPT can't generate a map of Europe*. Available at: https://cybernews.com/tech/chatgpt-cant-spell/ (Accessed: 10 December 2025)

Digital Silk (2025) AI Statistics in 2025: Key Trends and Usage Data. Available at: https://www.digitalsilk.com/digital-trends/ai-statistics/ (Accessed: 10 December 2025)

Exploding Topics (2025) *How Many Companies Use AI? (New 2025 Data)*. Available at: https://explodingtopics.com/blog/companies-using-ai (Accessed: 10 December 2025)

Fellow (2025) 'Meetings statistics: how many hours do we spend in meetings?', *Fellow Blog*, 10 December. Available at: https://fellow.ai/blog/meetings-statistics-how-many-hours-do-we-spend-in-meetings/ (Accessed: 12 December 2025)

Fortune (2025) *Deloitte was caught using AI in $290,000 report to help the Australian government—and it backfired*. Available at: https://fortune.com/2025/10/07/deloitte-ai-australia-government-report-hallucinations-technology-290000-refund/ (Accessed: 11 December 2025)

Hall, R. (2025) 'Google edits Super Bowl ad for AI that featured false information', *The Guardian*, 6 February. Available at: https://www.theguardian.com/technology/2025/feb/06/google-edits-super-bowl-ad-for-ai-that-featured-false-information (Accessed: 12 December 2025)

Kneese, T. (2024) 'Carbon emissions in the tailpipe of generative AI', *Harvard Data Science Review*. Available at: https://hdsr.mitpress.mit.edu/pub/fscsqwx4 (Accessed: 11 December 2025)

Madigan, S., McArthur, B.A., Elkhodary, R. et al. (2024) 'Screen time and parent–child talk when children are aged 12 to 36 months', *JAMA Pediatrics*. Available at: https://pmc.ncbi.nlm.nih.gov/articles/PMC10913002/ (Accessed: 10 December 2025)

Mark, G., Gonzalez, V.M. and Harris, J. (2005) 'No task left behind? Examining the nature of fragmented work', in *Proceedings of the SIGCHI Conference on Human Factors in Computing Systems (CHI '05)*. New York: ACM Press

Meta (2023) *Facebook Today and Tomorrow*. Meta Newsroom, 8 March. Available at: https://about.fb.com/news/2023/03/facebook-today-and-tomorrow/ (Accessed: 10 December 2025)

Microsoft (2023) *Microsoft 2023 Annual Report* and related communications. Available at: https://www.microsoft.com/investor/reports/ar23/ (Accessed: 10 December 2025)

Miller, H. (2025) 'Council tax typo costs authority £200,000', *BBC News*, 3 November. Available at: https://www.bbc.co.uk/news/articles/c051066d523o (Accessed: 10 December 2025)

Molson Coors Beverage Company (2025) 'Coors Light statement on misspelled ads', *Business Wire*, 13 January. Available at: https://www.businesswire.com/news/home/20250113272813/en/Coors-Light-Statement-on-Misspelled-Ads (Accessed: 12 December 2025)

National Literacy Trust (2024) *Children and young people's reading in 2024*. London: National Literacy Trust. Available at: https://literacytrust.org.uk/research-services/research-reports/children-and-young-peoples-reading-in-2024/ (Accessed: 10 December 2025)

Neath, A. (2025) 'Network Rail tells staff to stop saying passenger in bid to "speak customer's language"', *The Independent*, 3 February. Available at: https://www.independent.co.uk/travel/news-and-advice/network-rail-passengers-communication-guidance-b2691031.html (Accessed: 12 December 2025)

News18 (2025) 'Why has Puma changed its spelling to "PVMA" on store boards?', *News18*, 13 January. Available at: https://www.news18.com/viral/why-has-puma-changed-its-spelling-to-pvma-on-store-boards-ws-ab-9188616.html (Accessed: 12 December 2025)

Niederhoffer, K., Rosen Kellerman, G., Lee, A., Liebscher, A., Rapuano, K. and Hancock, J.T. (2025) 'AI-generated "workslop" is destroying productivity', *Harvard Business Review*, 24 September. Available at: https://hbr.org/2025/09/ai-generated-workslop-is-destroying-productivity (Accessed: 10 December 2025)

Onrec (2025) '1 in 2 job applicants use AI tools to help write CVs', *Onrec*, 14 May. Available at: https://www.onrec.com/news/statistics/1-in-2-job-applicants-use-ai-tools-to-help-write-cvs (Accessed: 12 December 2025)

Paphitis, T. (2025) *Dyslexia isn't a weakness. It's a different way of seeing the world* [LinkedIn post], 10 November. Available at: https://www.linkedin.com/posts/theopaphitis_dyslexia-isnt-a-weakness-its-a-different-activity-7386650080117751808-y8Qy (Accessed: 10 December 2025)

Radicati Group (2021) *Email Statistics Report, 2021–2025: Executive Summary*. Palo Alto, CA: The Radicati Group, Inc. Available at: https://www.radicati.com/wp/wp-content/uploads/2021/04/Email-Market-2021-2025-Executive-Summary.pdf (Accessed: 10 December 2025)

Río, S. (2025) 'Is your next hire real? Detecting AI-generated résumés and augmenting the modern recruiter', SergioRio.tech, 2 July. Available at: https://sergiorio.tech/flow/authenticity-arms-race-detecting-ai-generated-resumes-and-augmenting-the-modern-recruiter *(Accessed: 12 December 2025)*

Runn (2024) *Time management statistics: understand where your time really goes at work*. Available at: https://www.runn.io/blog/time-management-statistics (Accessed: 10 December 2025)

Sender.net (2025) '40+ latest call to action statistics for 2025', *Sender Blog*, 1 September. Available at: https://www.sender.net/blog/call-to-action-statistics/ (Accessed: 12 December 2025)

Talbot, J.M. (2020) 'Together, apart with emojis?', *Virality: A&SM 4.5* [online]. Available at: https://viralcontagion.blog/wp-content/uploads/2020/07/asm-4-5_johanna-talbot.pdf (Accessed: 11 December 2025)

The Reading Agency (2024) *About us*. Available at: https://www.charityjob.co.uk/organisation/read—the-reading-agency-ltd (Accessed: 10 December 2025)

Thomas, R. (2025) 'France rejects four-tonne oyster haul over "typo"', *BBC News*, 25 September. Available at: https://www.bbc.com/news/articles/c1kwpv9177jo (Accessed: 10 December 2025)

Tuckman, B.W. (1965) 'Developmental sequence in small groups', *Psychological Bulletin*, 63(6), pp. 384–399

Tuckman, B.W. and Jensen, M.A.C. (1977) 'Stages of small-group development revisited', *Group & Organization Studies*, 2(4), pp. 419–427

Worldometer (2025) *World Population Clock: 8.2 Billion People (LIVE)*. Available at: https://www.worldometers.info/world-population/ (Accessed: 10 December 2025)

Index

Printed and bound by CPI Group (UK) Ltd, Croydon, CR0 4YY

07/07/2026

02159992-0004